Simplified Sesh Medew Netcher Penmanship

Simplified Sesh Medew Netcher Penmanship
A Lesson in Egyptian Hieroglyphic Writing
Book One: Monoliterals

Emykhet Akhu Kinshaye Akinyi

Simplified Sesh Medew Netcher Penmanship
A Lesson in Egyptian Hieroglyphic Writing
Book One: Monoliterals

A Heka Multimedia Press Book
www.hekamultimedia.com

Cover photo: Image of scribe (Rosicrucian Park, San Jose, CA)

Cover Design by Wudjau Men-Ib Iry-Ma'at

Printed and bound in the United States of America

First Edition

ISBN-13: 978-0692974681
ISBN-10: 0692974687

To my grandmother, Petronala Akoth Opany Nyakamreri.

Table of Contents

List of Illustrations

Acknowledgments

To my mother, Sweety, and family for their love and guidance. To Wudjau Men-Ib iry-Maat for being a beautiful part of my life and growth. Family of colleagues, Seshew Maa Ny Medew Netcher: Antwon Jermain Clark, Djehuti Ma'at, Setepenra Meri Amen, Robert H. Allen Jr., Kofie Piesie, Christopher Knowles, Atiba Seku, Damiyon "Damo" Everly, Ini-Herit Shawn Khalfani and Wudjau Men-Ib Iry-Maat. Gratitude to the elders: Dr. Rhkty Amen, Dr. Theophile Obenga, Dr. Cheikh Anta Diop (29 December 1923 - 7 February 1986), Jean-Claude Mboli, Mfundishi Jhutymus Ka N Heru El-Salim for their contribution of information on cultures and languages of Africa. Recognition to the works of University of Kemet Press, the Amen Ra Squad (Ankhkakek, Sonjedi, Asar Imhotep, Wudjau, Nyah Amara, Jonathan Owens, Benjamin Njie and Nehisi). I give thanks to the continued support from Stan Knight, Stephen Ogongo and Vioxii Dede. A special thanks to those who continue to support me not mentioned here and the future Aspiring Scribes of the Divine Words.

Preface

Literacy (the ability to read and write) is something that any language student attains to acquire. For those wishing to learn the ancient Egyptian hieroglyphic writing system, reading and writing are in fact the only two modalities at their disposal out of the four namely, reading, listening (**receptive**), writing and speaking (**productive**). They are also quite sufficient as they fill both ends of the spectrum. But, gaining the skill to write the script may seem unattainable especially for those who may not feel "artistically" inclined.

As a calligrapher, I have learned that letters are broken down to their basic strokes and then built back up by connecting them to form their shapes. The understanding of forms and the best mechanical processes required to execute them is what makes the best scribes and penmen of our time and of the past. When one has mastered these techniques, forming desired shapes become intuitive. This is the inspiration behind the creation of this book which is to be utilized as a resource to help those who wish to learn the art of writing hieroglyphs in a straight forward and effortless manner.

The script of choice is cursive hieroglyphic or Simplified Sesh Medew Netcher used by the scribes of ancient Egypt. The handwritten script allows for a quicker and simpler method of notation as there are less number of strokes needed to complete a hieroglyphic drawing. This book contains finely detailed illustrations showing each step required to form the hieroglyphs and the best method of scribing them accurately and efficiently. Also included are additional information regarding the hieroglyphic writing system, the art of writing and drawing, and basic instructions on penmanship: tools and techniques.

Introduction

Penmanship was very important to the scribes of ancient Egypt. They were the literate group of the society and were pivotal in the Egyptian bureaucracy. The ability to read and write not only granted them administrative positions, but also knowledge of the divine words and cultivation of good moral conduct. The scribes were the model to which success and achievement was measured. For those who dedicated themselves to writing, their names were assured to last for eternity when read out loud through scrolls long after their demise. Indeed, through the writings of these record keepers of ancient Egyptians day to day life, we have been able to collect abundant knowledge of the civilization's rich history.

Today, writing by hand has become somewhat of a dying art form. It has been replaced by typing which is preferred for its speed and flexibility. But for those undertaking the day to day task of **Sesh Medew Netcher** (hieroglyphic) notation, this statement could be far from the truth. Handwriting or scribing hieroglyphs is still far more convenient, quicker and flexible as opposed to the task of inputing and editing them digitally. Obstacles typically arise from the lack of scribal skills. It is for this reason that competency in Sesh Medew Netcher scribing cannot be overlooked in any serious curriculum designed to prepare its students in the language acquisition. It should serve the student well to be just as skilled in writing as he or she is in the reading of the writing system.

It is common for students to spend a good amount of time attempting to draw elaborate hieroglyphs as part of their note taking process. This is neither productive nor practical. How would one labor through the scribing of simple phrases let alone full texts utilizing this approach? Writing regardless of the script used should be rapid and intuitive. It should augment the flow of thought and speech.

For the ancient Egyptian scribes, a clear distinction was made between the script used to adorn the walls of pyramids and tombs and those that were handwritten on papyri etc. Cursive hieroglyphic also known as **Simplified Sesh Medew Netcher** is one of the handwritten scripts used by the scribes of ancient Egypt. It retained some of the hieroglyphic pictorial nature from which the signs derive. Using the script, scribes were able to write more quickly as the outline style of drawing allowed for the use of less number of strokes to complete a hieroglyphic drawing. It is this need for a writing style that is quick, simple and authentic to the scripts of Ancient Egypt that led to the conception of this book. This book aims at providing an easy-to-understand, detailed guide on how to scribe Simplified Sesh Medew Netcher for practical day to day writing. One will also find that this script provides for an easy transition towards a better understanding of the more cursive style of writing known as **Sesh Medjat Netcher** (Hieratic): Some of the hieroglyphs from Simplified Sesh Medew Netcher are either shared or slightly detailed versions of their Sesh Medjat Netcher counterparts.

How To Use This Book

This book is dedicated to the single consonantal signs known as **monoliterals**. The monoliterals contain all the possible known sounds in the language. On their own, they can be used to write any hieroglyphic word combination (they were never used as such by the Ancient Egyptians but rather to help spell out other signs in words). The ability to commit the set of monoliteral hieroglyphs to memory is also a basic requirement when undertaking the study of the writing system. Learning how to scribe them aids in this endeavor. For these reasons, it is a logical starting point.

It should be noted that this book is aimed at teaching you how to write Simplified Sesh Medew Netcher monoliterals. There is no attempt to give extensive explanations into the language and its grammar. For those, both the Beginner's and Grammar books by **Wudjau Men-Ib Iry-Maat** are recommended.

The first section of the book presents some basic information regarding the Hieroglyphic writing system, the different styles of writing, scribes, their tools and methods of training.

The second section examines the art of writing and drawing. Here, the drawing and writing process is demystified by breaking down and helping you recognize their underlying fundamentals in an easy and manageable format. Also included in this section are basic instructions on penmanship tools and techniques you will need to perfect your skill.

The last section of the book focuses on how to write each monoliteral sign. Illustrations are provided showing you each step of forming the hieroglyphs and the method of scribing them accurately and efficiently.

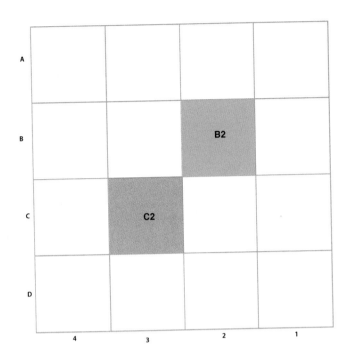

Illustrations of the hieroglyphs are done in a 4*4 grid block. For easy identification of squares within the grid, columns are numbered **1 - 4** from right to left and rows marked as **ABCD** from top to bottom. There are 16 equal squares within the grid. When discussing individual squares, each is labeled in relation to its row and column position.

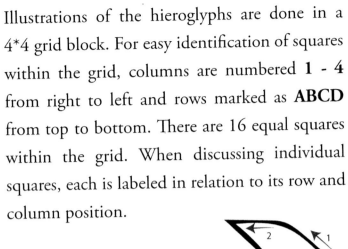

Red arrows indicate the directional flow of lines drawn to form the glyph. This is not to be mistaken for the number of separate strokes or pen lift positions present within the glyph.

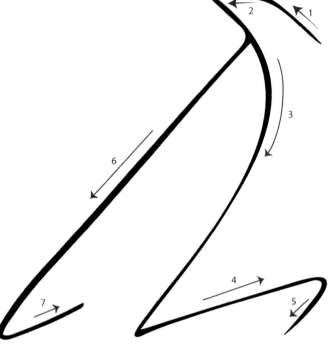

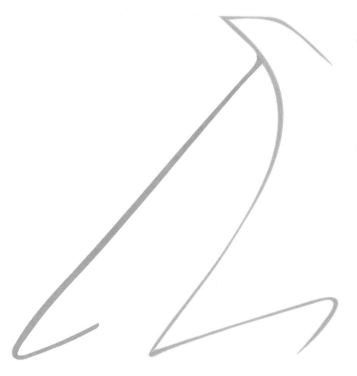

Multicolored illustrations indicate the different strokes present within a glyph. For example, the blue section is drawn in one continuous stroke. The same applies to the orange section. This indicates that there are only two strokes in this glyph. The pen is lifted only once from the paper in order to execute the hieroglyph drawing.

Terminology

The following are words used throughout this book that may differ to what is commonly used by Egyptologists.

Common	This Book
Egypt	Kemet
Kemetic	Kemety
Egyptian	Nykemet
Egyptian People	Remetch
Spoken Egyptian Language	RanyKemet
Written Egyptian Language	Sesh Medew Netcher

The methods used throughout this book when referring to words in Sesh Medew Netcher will be given in four parts as: <signs>, <transliteration>, <Egyptology pronunciation>, and <meaning>. For example, $m\underline{d}3t$ 'medjat' « papyrus roll » where:

The signs are represented as themselves -

Transliteration is in italic -$m\underline{d}3t$

Egyptology pronunciation is enclosed in single quotation marks - 'medjat'

Meaning is enclosed in double arrows - « papyrus roll »

Complementary Website

www.mdw-ntr.com

Although this book is a stand alone learning tool, a complementary website has been created to assist in the learning process. The goal of the website is to provide everything needed to learn the language of ancient Kemet - *sš mdw-nṯr* (Sesh Medew Netcher). It provides study courses, articles related to language and Kemet in general, pictures of Egyptian artefacts, and a wealth of resources to assist in learning the language. The study courses are available for access to online interaction with an instructor and others learning in a step by step fashion along with additional exercises in transliterations, translations and scribing.

Materials available on the website.

- Customized grid papers made in rows and columns for easy scribing. For the right scribing practice to be developed from the early stages, it is recommend that scribing is done on grid paper. Using a square as a reference helps correctly balance the glyph proportions and give aesthetically pleasing results.

- Additional instructions on the use of brushes, reed and dip pens. For those that may want to experiment with using different writing implements other than the fountain pen.

- Additional drills and exercises.

CHAPTER 1

1. Hieroglyphic Writing system

1.1 Writing Systems

Writing has provided us with the means to communicate and store information. This information can be retrieved unaltered after a long period of time without the need of the original writer's presence. Of course, we now live in a world where technologies such as voice recorders are used to store speech, but the written word still remains the most ubiquitous medium of information storage.

Writing can be defined as the graphical representation of a spoken language. A writing system contains a set of signs that make up its script. The words in different spoken languages can be represented using one writing system or script. For example, the Roman script is used to represent the spoken languages of English, Spanish and German. On the other hand, one spoken language can be written using multiple writing systems. For example, Swahili an African Bantu language is graphically represented using both the Arabic and the Roman script.

Just as in the spoken language, messages encoded in a script can only be decoded if both the writer and the reader have a shared understanding of the meanings behind the set of characters making up the script.[1] In short, you are able to read the written words in this book and understand the messages behind them because you have knowledge of the **writing system** used and the **spoken language** it represents. But what happens in instances where an unknown writing system to a known or partially known language is found and we need to understand its message? In such cases, the process of decipherment is applied.

1.2 Decipherment Of The Hieroglyphic Writing System

Decipherment is the process of elucidating the relationship between a writing system and the spoken language it represents. For centuries the decipherment of the hieroglyphic had eluded many historians of antiquity such as Horapollo (ca 400CE) and Athanasius Kircher (1601/1602-1680 CE) who viewed the writing system as purely pictorial symbols of magic. Not until a proper understanding of the hieroglyphic was gained, did decipherment take place.

---

[1]   Seshew Maa Ny Medew Netcher, *Has the Egyptian Hieroglyphic Writing System Been Deciphered? - A Rebuttal to Walter Williams,* 2016, p. 10-11

Champollion is credited for deciphering the hieroglyphs but, it should be noted that no successful decipherment of ancient scripts has been done by a single individual. It is a process that takes an accumulative amount of minds and many years or decades to accomplish. Some of the scholars who's efforts led to the decipherment of the hieroglyphs include, Sylvester de Sacy, Johan Åkerblad, Thomas Young and finally Champollion. The Rosetta and Canopus stones were some of the artefacts instrumental in the decipherment process. After Champollion's death, other scholars notably Karl Richard Lepsius used his system to successfully decipher new inscriptions.[2] From the success of the decipherment, we are now able to have glimpses of the Ancient Egyptians and their society through the texts and other materials excavated.

1.3 Sesh Medew Netcher

Kemet (Ancient Egypt) was one of the first civilizations to invent a writing system that flourished for over three thousand years. The writing system as a whole used by the **Remetch** (Ancient Egyptians) is known as **Sesh Medew Netcher** which translates to Inscriptions of Divine Words or what is commonly known as Hieroglyphic. Each sign within the writing system is referred to as a hieroglyph. The English use of the term hieroglyph comes from late Latin hieroglyphicus which is from the Greek adjective ἱερογλυφικός hieroglyphikos, a compound of two Greek words, ἱερός hieros - 'sacred' + γλύφω glyphein - 'to carve.' The writing system along with the spoken language, **Ranykemet**, underwent various changes with the hieroglyphs expanding from roughly 700 signs in use during the Old and Middle Kingdom to approximately 7000 signs by the Greco Roman Period.

Sesh Medew Netcher signs are pictorial in form and visually represents images of natural flora, fauna and man made objects indigenous to the Nile Valley Corridor. A pictographic sign represents the physical object it signifies. For instance, this ☀ pictographic sign signifies the sun. The sign conveys the same message regardless of the different languages spoken by the readers. Pictographs are however limited to physical objects in our surrounding. How then would we visually represent non tangible objects? In time, this ☀ pictograph would have developed into an ideograph like this ☉ representing a non tangible object or concept and idea such as, 'heat' or 'day'.

Ibid., p. 23, 74-80, 84-85, 103-104

1.4 Functions of Signs

Pictographs and ideographs on their own are not sufficient enough to make up a writing system. A writing system has two main features: signs with sound value and signs with meaning value. Sesh Medew Netcher signs are pictographs which function in one of these three roles:

Logograph - These are signs that function as graphic representations of specific morphemes, words or phrases in a language. Sesh Medew Netcher logographs are typically written with an additional vertical stroke indicating that the sign is read as a whole word. Examples: 𓄣 *ỉb* 'eeb' « heart/mind » and 𓉐 *pr* "per" « house ».

Phonograph - These are signs representing sounds of the language. They spell out words. Phonographs can be **monoliteral** signs representing one consonant, **biliteral** signs representing two consonants or **triliteral** signs representing three consonants. Below are some examples.

Monoliterals

Signs	Code	Description	Diacritic	MdC
𓇋	M17	reed leaf	*ỉ*	i
𓅱	G43	quail chick	*w*	w
𓂋	D21	mouth	*r*	r

Biliterals

Signs	Code	Description	Diacritic	MdC
𓌀	U23	chisel	*ꜣb*	Ab
𓏠	Y5	game board	*mn*	mn
𓁷	D2	face	*ḥr*	Hr

Triliterals

Signs	Code	Description	Diacritic	MdC
⸙	M17	sandle-strap	*ꜥnḫ*	anx
⸌	G43	raised standard	*nṯr*	nTr
⸔	D21	loaf on mat	*ḥtp*	Htp

Determinative - These are mute signs with no phonetic value. They serve as classifiers determining the semantic scope of words they are attached to. Since they appear at the end of a word, they are also used to determine word separation as there are no spaces to mark word clusters. Below are examples of four words with the verb *wn* 'wen' exist: that otherwise appear the same except for their determinatives which help identify their semantic range.

	wn « open » (door - ⟳)
	wn « hurry » (legs in motion - ⋀)
	wn « fault, blame » (sparrow - ⟿)
	wn « stripped off » (hair - ⟆)

1.5 Reading Direction

Hieroglyphs can be written and read in four different directions:

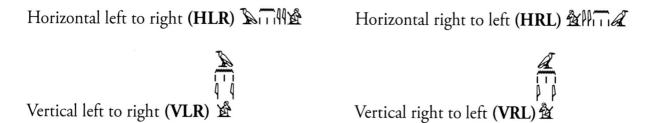

Horizontal left to right (**HLR**)

Horizontal right to left (**HRL**)

Vertical left to right (**VLR**)

Vertical right to left (**VRL**)

The reading direction is determined by looking at the direction in which animate signs such as birds, people and animals are facing such that if they are written facing left, then the text is read from left to right. Exception to this rule is found in **retrograde** inscriptions where the signs face the end of the inscription. When reading in any of the four directions, signs on top are always read first.

1.6 Order of Signs

The order of signs were sometimes reversed or misspelled by scribes. This was done for one of these two reasons:

Honorific transposition: this occurs when names referring to kings or deities precede in a phrases or compound words although they are actually read afterwards. It is commonly found in epithets and titles. Example: The phrase *mdw nṯr* 'medew netcher' «divine words» 𓊹𓌃 where the glyph 𓊹 'netcher' « divine » precedes when written but comes after when read.

Graphic transposition: This occurs for aesthetic reasons. Words are misspelled in-order to preserve proportionality in grouped signs.

Example: The word *nḥḥ* 'neheh' « eternity » is written as 𓇓𓇳𓇓 instead of the formal 𓈖𓎛𓎛𓇳

1.7 Grids and Quadrats

Scribes adhered to an orderly, proportioned arrangement of glyphs in their scribal methods by making use of **quadrat blocks.** Quadrat blocks are imaginary square or rectangular guidelines used by scribes to arrange signs in-order to achieve symmetry (see fig 2.5).

1.8 Shapes of Glyphs

The arrangement of Sesh Medew Netcher signs are dependent on the shape of each individual sign. Every sign has one of these three basic shapes: **tall narrow** signs, **flat broad** signs and **low narrow** signs. Tall narrow signs typically stand by themselves while flat broad and low narrow signs are usually arranged into square or rectangular groups (see the appendix).

Glyphs within a 4 *4 grid when scribing

Tall narrow signs cover the entire four rows in height and one column in width but can extend up to two columns in width.

Low broad signs cover one row in height and the entire four columns in width. Some low broad signs can extend up to two rows in height.

Low narrow signs cover up to two rows in height and two columns in width.

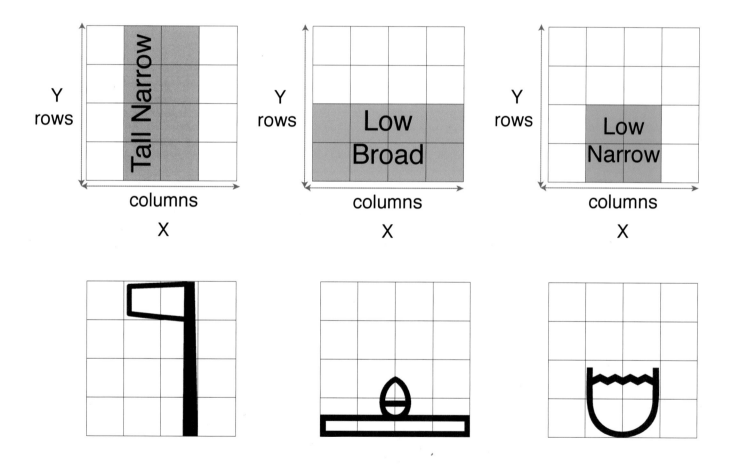

Fig 1.1

1.9 Styles of Writing

Two forms of Sesh Medew Netcher were used concurrently. Formal Sesh Medew Netcher, the very detailed pictorials inscribed as carvings on monuments, paintings on tombs, etc and the simplified styles of writing used by scribes for the urgency of storing the day to day records. These simplified styles included:

- **Simplified Sesh Medew Netcher** (Cursive),

- **Sesh Medjat Netcher** (Hieratic),

- **Sesh Ny Shat** (Demotic) and

- **Coptic.**

Simplified Sesh Medew Netcher otherwise known as cursive by Egyptologists is a simpler form of the elaborate formal Sesh Medew Netcher found on the wall carvings and tombs paintings. It was written with the use of reed brushes and ink on papyri, wood or leather. This style of writing is almost exclusively found in religious texts known as *rw nw prt m hrw*, translated as *Utterances For Coming Forth By Day* (Book Of the Dead). It exhibits a drawing style of outlines that still kept the distinct characteristics of the various images intact. The number of strokes or pen lifts needed to draw the hieroglyphs were also reduced in the pursuit of speed (see fig. 1.2). The texts were mostly written in columns from right to left using black and red ink. Simplified Sesh Medew Netcher will be the core style used in this penmanship course.

Other Simplified Styles

The various styles of simplification led to even more cursive and abstract styles of writings such as **Sesh Medjat Netcher** or Hieratic (see fig 1.3) and **Sesh ny Shat** (Demotic). These two styles defer from Simplified Sesh Medew Netcher in that the signs are more abstract and contain **ligatures**.[3] Sesh ny Shat is exclusively written from right to left.

---

3   Ligatures are made when two signs are connected together.

Fig 1.2

Fig 1.3

Towards the first Century AD, those who adopted Christianity began using the Coptic script to translate the sacred scriptures of the new religion. The Coptic alphabet has thirty-two letters: twenty-four taken from Greek, seven for sounds that Egyptian had but Greek did not, and one monogram (one letter standing for two).

*Sections **1.3** to **1.9** contain excerpts taken from, **A Beginner's Introduction to Medew Netcher** (2015) by Wudjau Men-Ib Iry Maat.*

1.10 Scribes

The word 𓏞 *sš* 'sesh' « scribe » is attributed to one who writes and the act of writing or drawing. The two patron deities of scribes are 𓋇 *sš3t* 'Seshat' « Seshat » the female who is "foremost in the house of books" and 𓅝 *dḥwty* 'Djehuty' « Djehuty or Thoth », "lord of Medew Netcher." Scribes wrote and kept the records found on papyri, wall carvings and paintings in tombs and coffins. Their writings has provided us with the means of acquiring direct evidence of the history of Kemet. Scribes were the literate group in the society occupying every area of its administration. As small a number as they were, they influenced a great deal of its state bureaucracy. They organized the military and priesthood, calculated tax dues, recorded court proceedings and legal contracts among other duties.

Theirs was the most sought after office. In the "Teachings of Duwaw-Khety" also known as "The Satire of Trades", the scribe Duwaw Khety sailing south to **the Residence** to place his son Pepy in the 𓂑𓏠𓊹𓂇𓏛 *ct sb3 nt sšw* 'at seba net seshew' « **school of scribes** » among the children of officials, instructs his son on the importance of scribal duties stating: *"it is greater than any office, there is none like it on earth."* [4] In the text, scribal duty is exalted in contrast to what is considered as laborious trades of the carpenters, brick layers, craftsmen, farmers etc. Such manual labor could be eluded by the aspiring scribe through his dedication to writing. Copious numbers of other texts or instructions were written in praise of the scribal profession. In the papyrus Lansing (Obenga, 2004), the student was encouraged to *"cherish study, avoid the dance, so you'll become an excellent official."* He was advised to *"not yearn after outdoor pleasures, hunting and fishing; shun boomerang throwing and the chase."* Instead, he was to *"write diligently by day; and recite at night."* The teachings reminded him, *"let your friends be the papyrus roll and scribal palette; such work is sweeter than wine."* [5] The importance and prestige of scribal profession is seen in the statues of high officials that were made in the famous scribal sitting posture. It became synonymous with one of high status.

Such a prestigious office was not easy to attain. Apprenticeship was primarily through father and son where the son inherited his father's position. However, it was not uncommon for some scribes to advance from humble beginnings to such ranks. It should be noted that not all identification of

---

4   Stephen Quirke, *Egyptian Literature 1800 BC, questions and readings,* London Golden House Publications Egyptology 2, 2004, p. 121

5   Theophile Obenga, *African Philosophy, The Pharaonic Period: 2780-330 BC* Per Ankh Publishing, 2004, p 243-247

"son" was literal. A scribe would sometimes refer to his pupil as his son. In most cases the biological son was identified as "of ones own body" or seed.[6]

1.11 Instructions

sb3yt "Sebayeet" « Instructions » for the young aspiring scribes was overseen at a special *ˁt sb3* 'at seba' « school » in the palace or temple.[7] Learning began with the Sesh Medjat Netcher script. These instructions included the tracing and recitation of cursive literary texts from classic teachings (Instructions of Duwaw Khety, Ptahhotep etc.) And the compendium known as *kmyt* 'kemyeet' « book of completion ». The kemyt (see Fig 1.4), consisted of Middle Egyptian compilations of phrases and formulae used throughout the New Kingdom.[8] It was typically written in a style closer to Simplified Sesh Medew Netcher arranged in columns.

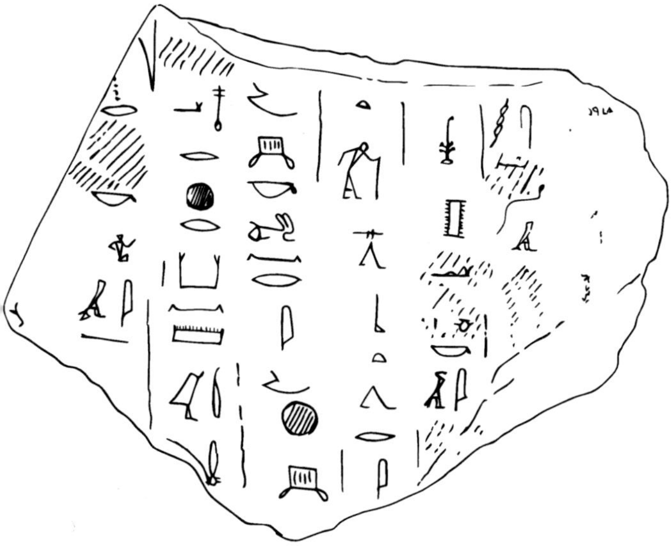

Fig 1.4

Some of the subjects taught included, grammar, spelling, mathematics, geometry, letter-writing and onomastics.[9] Onomasticons were classification list indicating the categories into which the Remetch divided the world. The Onomasticon of Amenemope is known to contain a complete list of 610 words.[10]

6 Ronald J Williams, *Scribal Training in Ancient Egypt,* JAOS Vol. 92, No. 2, 1972, p. 215

7 Ibid, p. 216

8 Christopher Eyre and John Baines, *Interactions between Orality and Literacy in Ancient Egypt,* Karen Schousboe and Mogens. Trolle Larsen (eds), *Literacy and Society* (Copenhagen, 1989), New York, London, Oxford University Press, Inc, 1947, p. 95

9 Donald B Redford, ed., *The Oxford Encyclopedia of Ancient Egypt, vol 1,* New York,. Oxford University Press, Inc, 2001, p. 439-441

10 Alan H Gardiner, *Ancient Egyptian Onomastica, vol. 1,* New York, London, Oxford University Press, Inc, 1947, p. 37

Instructions commenced from the learning of words and complete phrases progressing through different lines until the texts was completed.[11] Instructions also had the dual purpose of imparting proper moral conduct for the scribes. For the unruly student engaging in disrespectful activities, disciplinary actions such as floggings also known as 𓏏𓃀𓇼𓏏 *sbȝyt* 'Sebayeet' « punishment » was administered.

After elementary class studies, some students received the title 𓏞 *sš* 'sesh' « scribe » and advanced to higher classes, while others proceeded to complete their final years of scribal training serving as an apprentice 𓅱𓂝 *ḥry-ꜥ* 'hery a' « boy or youngster, » under the supervision of a master.[12]

1.12 Female Scribes

Although no records have been found of appointed female scribes tasked with the recording of official documents etc, the tutoring of some elite women may have been done privately such as is the case with Hatshepsut's daughter Neferura who is known to have been under the tutelage of the scribe Senenmut. Senenmut bore the title "Steward of the King's Daughter" as a reference to Neferura.[13]

1.13 Scribal Implements

Scribes had a portable scribal kit known as 𓏠 *mnhḏ* 'Menehedj' « scribe's palette » The kit included:

- A rectangular shaped palette board, made of either wood, ivory or stone with two ink pans for red and black ink. The black ink was from charcoal or soot. Red ink was made from ochre. The red ink was used to highlight important passages, titles, headings and the start of new sections. It was also used by teachers to correct mistakes made by students. Palettes with more than two pans were not uncommon and some also had a slot to hold sharpened reeds for writing.

---

11   Baines and Eyre, *Interaction Between Orality and Literacy in Ancient Egypt,* p. 95
12   Williams, *Scribal Training in Ancient Egypt,* p. 215
13   Ibid, p. 220

- Mortar and pestle for grinding ink pigments.

- Water pots for mixing liquids and ink pigments.

- Burnishing stone and knife for smoothing sheets of papyrus before writing.

For learning or practicing, aspiring scribes often used broken potsherds known as **ostracons**. They were cheap, plentiful, durable and reusable. Papyrus was reserved for official documents as it was costly. It was made from cut strips from the papyrus plant layered on top of each other at right angles and soaked until the natural adhesives in the plant fiber held the strips together. It was then pressed, dried and smoothed to create a smooth writing surface.

1.14 Types of Scribes

Scribes held different offices or titles in Kemet. Some of their occupations included reading letters on behalf of the people who could not read, serving as painters and draughtsmen, working in the military etc. Below is a list of some of the titles held by scribes:

- 𓏞𓎭 *sš ḥsb* 'Sesh Heseb' « Scribe of Accounts » who kept records of grain supplies etc.

- 𓏞𓃀𓏤𓏤 *sš ḳdwt* 'Sesh Kedweet' « scribe of outline or draughtsman »

- 𓇓𓏞 *sš nswt* 'Sesh Nesuw' « Royal scribe »

- 𓏞�𓏤𓏜𓏲 *sš dnit* 'Sesh Deneet' « Scribe of distribution »

- 𓏞�\u200b𓏤𓃀 *sš šꜥt* 'Sesh Shat' « Secretary or letter writers »

- 𓏞𓌪 *sš mšꜥ* 'Sesh Mesew' « Army Scribe »

- 𓏞𓏥𓏤𓃀𓈖 *sš sḫn* 'Sesh Sekhen' « Administrative Scribe »

- 𓏞𓉐𓊹 *sš ḥwt nṯr* "Sesh Hewut Netcher" « Scribe of the Temple »

Exercise 1

1.   The Remetch referred to their writing system as:

    A.   Hieroglyphicus

    B.   Sesh Medew Netcher

    C.   Medew Netcher

    D.   Ranykemet

2.   In what direction is this phrase read in? 𓅓𓃀𓏤𓏤𓊖𓈖𓏤𓅓𓂋𓈖𓊖

    A.   Horizontal left to right (HLR)

    B.   Horizontal right to left (HRL

    C.   Vertical left to right (VLR)

    D.   Vertical right to left (VRL)

3.   Scribes were free to arrange signs in any way they deemed appropriate.

    A.   True

    B.   False

4.   Simplified Sesh Medew Netcher contains ligatures?

      A.   True

      B.   False

5.   What is the name of 'instructions' undertaken by aspiring scribes in ancient Egypt?

      A.   *sbꜣyt*

      B.   *šꜥt n sbꜣ*

      C.   *sš*

      D.   *sꜣ*

CHAPTER 2

2. Tools and Techniques

2.1 Drawing vs Writing

When looking at the image ☀ and the word *'sun'* we are able to distinguish the difference between that which is **drawn** from that which is **written**. They differ in their visual form and symbolic function even though they are designated to the same referent. One is a realistic visual representation of the object. Its meaning is derived from the similarities between its form and the object it refers to. The word 'sun' is a set of abstract graphical symbols representing the units of a spoken language designated to the referent. Even though the visual differences of both representations are obvious to us, the mechanical process undertaken when writing and drawing these two signs are otherwise similar.

Drawing can be defined as *"To make pictures or a picture of something with pencil pen or chalk (but not paint)..."* [14] Writing is defined as *"to make letters or numbers on a surface, especially using a pen or pencil..."* [15] Drawing and writing both refer to the marking of different shapes and forms but mainly defer in the type and variations of shapes produced (pictures and letters). When writing, the set of symbols or shapes are confined and conform within a fixed convention. Drawing on the other hand is expressed in an unlimited multitude of shapes and forms that are in likeness of things or persons. [16] A penman and an artist both master the use of similar writing implements and must both be skilled in the production of ideal lines as a basic element in the production of different shapes or symbols. Johnson (1909: p, 62) defines the difference between an artist and a penman through the variety of shapes and forms each learns to perceive and execute. With this understanding, he explains that writing simply is the drawing of conventional (shapes or) forms. [17]

For the scribes in Kemet, the distinction between writing and drawing would appear to be greatly blurred, for the writing system utilized pictographic images as its set of signs or symbols. In order to write, a scribe had to learn how to draw. We observe this in the word 𓏟 *sš* 'sesh' which is used to denote both "write" and "draw". It is for this reason that a proper understanding of the fundamentals of writing and drawing are required for the mastery of Sesh Medew Netcher scribing.

14　　*Oxford Advanced Learner's Dictionary,* (8th ed), Oxford, New York, Oxford University Press, 2010, p.460

15　　Ibid, p.1785

16　　W. Martin Johnson, *The W. Martin Johnson school of art, Elementary Instruction In Color, Perspective, Lights and Shadows - pen drawing and composition,* New York, Library of Congress, 1909, p. 62

17　　Ibid

2.2 Art and Writing of Kemet

For the serious aspiring scribe, an artistic knowledge and understanding of forms is unavoidable. The art and writing of Kemet are closely related both having coexisted in the same domain functioning as tools for communicating the cultural and moral ideals of the Remetch.

Artists were well trained in observing conventions that kept the distinctive style and uniformity of Nykemet art. Certainly, as the hieroglyphs adhere to conventions which must be observed in order to decode them correctly, the laws governing the creation of Nykemet artistic images may also dictate and influence how we interpret them. To gain a complete understanding of the art, we not only appreciate them exclusively from an artistic point of view, but also draw from the understanding of the conventions observed in visually representing the standards of the Kemety culture.

Outside of their functions (phonographs, logographs and determinatives), the hieroglyphs can be viewed as pieces of art in their own right that are recognizable from the surrounding of the Remetch. On the other hand, art was occasionally used as large logographs representing objects of similar phonological structure to convey messages through the rebus principle. An example of this can be seen in the statue of king Rameses II depicting three symbols forming a rebus of his name *rꜥ-ms-sw* 'ramesew' where:

rꜥ is depicted as the solar disk on the child's head,

ms is the seated child and

sw is the sedge plant held by the child on his left hand.[18]

Fig. 2.1

---

18   Wudjau Men-Ib Iry-Maat, *A Beginner's Introduction to Medew Netcher,* 2nd ed., Heka Multimedia, 2015, p. 57

All images (statues, reliefs, etc.) were accompanied by texts either on the back pillar or the base identifying the individual depicted or utterances by the figure as seen on the statue of Rameses II (fig 2.1) where the base is carved with his royal titulary. When looking at inscriptions containing both texts (hieroglyphs) and images such as tomb paintings, we find that both the text and images (vignettes) complement each other in order to provide a complete interpretation of the recorded message. Here, the principles governing the use of determinatives can also be applied to the larger reliefs found in tomb walls and temples that accompany written texts. The images tend to function as large determinatives providing a broader semantic meaning of the inscription as a whole. This is akin to how determinatives preceding phonographs in written texts commonly function.

It is this flexibility that lent to the interrelationship and preservation of both the art and formal hieroglyphs as tools of conveying information.

2.3 Conventions of Kemety Art and Writing

Nykemet art did not capture that which was seen at a given time and space but rather, the essential characteristics of objects took precedence and encoded into forms governed by three elements namely; *Contour line, pictorial presentation* and *proportion* of which will be herein simplified as, **Outline, Aspective** and **Proportion**.[19] In the next section we will look at how these conventions were observed in the creation of both the art and writing.

2.4 The Outline

All art work began with the tracing of **outlines** [20] within which more detailed work would be applied by painters and sculptors.[21] The task of outlining was performed by the 𓏞𓏤𓆓𓈖𓏤 *sš ḳdwt* 'sesh kedweet'

---

19   Arthur Krispin, *An Overview of Ancient Egyptian Art* , Anistoriton Journal, section O054, Vol. 9, 2005

20   A line indicating the shape of an object

21   Stefanović Danijela, *sS qdwt – The Attestations from the Middle Kingdom and the Second Intermediate Period*, Budapest, Museum of Fine Arts, 2012, p. 185

« draughtsmen or outline scribes ». The word ⟨hieroglyphs⟩ *ḳdwt* 'kedweet' « drawings, sketches or outline figures » is derived from the root ⟨hieroglyphs⟩ *ḳd* 'qed' « to form » or ⟨hieroglyphs⟩ *ḳd* 'qed'« go around ». Outline markings by draughtsmen can be seen in unfinished reliefs found in tombs. The use of the outline as a base for further detailed work was also realized in the carvings and paintings of the elaborate hieroglyphs on walls and tomb paintings (Fig 2.4).

Fig. 2.2

The style used in Simplified Sesh Medew Netcher can be defined as outline drawings of its hieroglyphic counterparts with only the most notable characteristics left intact.[22] Fig 2.2 taken from plate 25 of *The papyrus of Ani*, show comparisons between the two (elaborate and cursive) styles of the G6 (combination of G5 and S45) determinative bik "falcon" with a flagellum. The outline is as an element identifiable and observed in both representations.

2.5 Aspective

The organization of shapes in space was different to what we are accustomed to today. Images were expressed using a composite of several views to show idealized features of objects in what Brunner-Traut (1974: p, 422.) terms as *"aspective"*. This is in contrast to perspective representation, where objects are depicted as is observed from one view point at a given time. As a rule in ancient Egyptian art, human figures were portrayed with their face in profile, the eye, shoulders and the torso in frontal view and the legs also shown in profile with the feet separated one from the other in order to show both. [23]

Fig. 2.3

22   E. A Wallis Budge, *Easy Lessons in Egyptian Hieroglyphics with Sign List, vol 3,* London, Routledge & Kegan Paul Ltd., 1973, p. 7

23   Gay Robins, *Proportion and Style in Ancient Egyptian Art,* Austin, TX, University of Texas Press, 1994, p. 13

The same principle of expressing objects was also applied to the hieroglyphs. In fig 2.3, the A2 hieroglyph representing the word *s* for man and also functioning as a determinative has the head in profile, torso twisted into a full frontal view and limbs positioned by employing conventions intended to show both legs.[24]

2.6 Proportion (Grids and Quadrat Blocks)

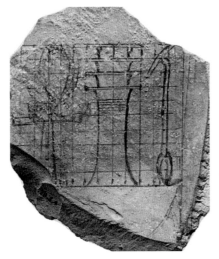

Fig. 2.4

In order to ensure a symmetrically balanced assemblage of body parts, draughtsmen sketched on squared grids as guidelines adhering to a set of fixed principles in what is known as **canon of proportions**. The grids also facilitated a means of copying and transferring sketches to different tomb walls.

The task of outlining was done by an apprentice in red paint and corrections by the master draughtsman was made in black for the final adaptation. The guidelines were then erased and further work applied.

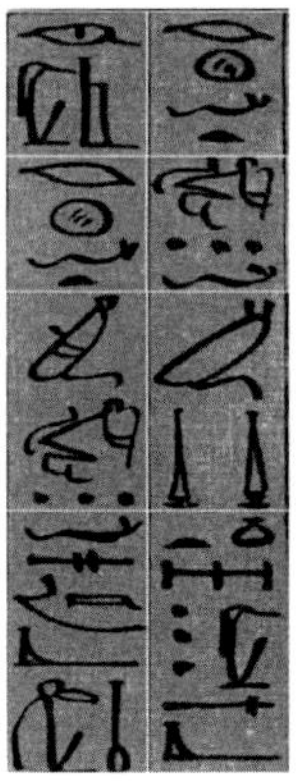

Hieroglyphs also adhered to a set of rules governing proportion. In the previous chapter, we learned that various signs occupy the space according to one of the three different types of shapes (tall narrow, flat broad, low narrow) they may take. Looking at the small portion taken from the *Papyrus of Ani* (fig 2.5), one may be puzzled to find objects such as the owl, vulture and even the reed leaf portrayed just as large as a seated human. The convention used follows that each hieroglyph is proportioned to itself.[25] The glyphs are then grouped to observe balance within the quadrat blocks.

Fig. 2.5

---

24   Richard H Wilkinson. *Reading Egyptian Art - A Hieroglyphic Guide to Ancient Egyptian Painting and Sculpture,* London: Thames and Hudson, 1992, p. 17

25   Schumann-Antelme and Rossini, *Illustrated Hieroglyphics Handbook, subsection - General Considerations on Hieroglyphic Writing,* New York, Sterling Publishing Co., Inc, 2002, p. 13

2.7 Outline Drawing

Outline can be described as the outer contour of an object. It is used to mark the basic character of any object and is the base to which all other secondary expressions are built upon. The words **Outline** and **Contour** are generally used interchangeably but it must be pointed out here that outline refers to the outer boundary indicating the shape or silhouette of an object while contour lines are used to describe not only the outer boundary but also the additional interior details of an object. (see Fig. 2.6). This is because not all contours of an object lie along its outline.

Fig. 2.6

2.8 Elements and Principles of Art

When drawing, artists are guided by rules that help convey their artwork as intended. They use ingredients known as **elements of art**. They are, *line, shape, form, space, value, color and texture*. The mechanisms of arranging and organizing these seven elements are known as **principles of art**. They are: *Pattern, Contrast, Emphasis, Balance, Harmony, Proportion/Scale and Rhythm/Movement*.

The following basic elements and principles of art are the essential components employed in outline drawing and thus the scribing of Simplified Sesh Medew Netcher. You will need to factor them in, when forming your hieroglyphs.

- Line
- Shape
- Space
- Proportion and Scale
- Balance

2.9 Art Elements

Line

A line is defined as the path of a moving point. It is perhaps the most essential element of writing and drawing. With lines, we are able to create familiar shapes and forms so as to express our ideas or what we see around us. Lines may vary in different ways but can be broken down into two types namely, **straight** lines and **curved** lines. Straight lines are made with no change in direction while curved lines are made with a continuous change in direction.[26]

Straight Lines

Straight lines can be made in three different directions. **Vertical** lines are drawn straight, up and down. **Horizontal** lines are drawn straight across, left and right. Both the vertical and horizontal lines never vary. **Oblique** lines are drawn in a slanting position and vary depending on their slant **angles**. These angles are measured in relation to the nearest horizontal and vertical line.

Angles in Straight Lines

An angle is the space in degrees between two lines at their meeting point. Examples of common angles are **acute angle** (less than 90 °), **right angle** (at 90°) and **obtuse angle** (larger than 90 °).

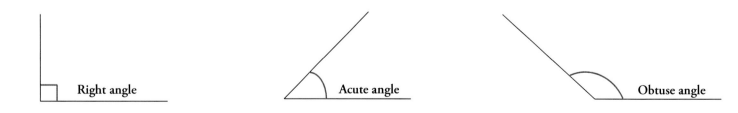

Right angle   Acute angle   Obtuse angle

Fig. 2.7

---

26   William Walker, *Handbook of drawing,* New York, C. Scribner's sons, 1880, p. 23

Curves

Although straight lines are simpler to make even in their variations, most objects in nature exhibit curves in their forms. The basic types of curves are: **circle, ellipse, oval** and **spiral**.[27]

Circle: every point of its outline or circumference, is of equal distant from the center.

Ellipse: is a squashed circle or a circle in perspective.

Oval: mimics the shape of an egg.

Spiral: start from a point and continuously widens or tightens as it revolves around the point.

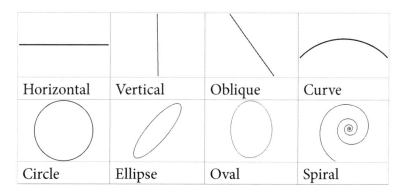

Fig. 2.8

Curvature

Curved lines have their directions constantly varying. The measure to which it deviates from a straight line is known as **curvature.** Tight curves have greater curvature while the curvature of a straight line can generally be defined to be at a constant zero.

27   Edmund J. Sullivan, *Line: An Art Study,* London, Chapman & Hall, Ltd., 1922, p.26

Compound Curves

When drawing, we encounter more complex shapes of curves than just circles, ellipses and ovals. The curves found in natural objects consists of combinations of different curves known as **compound curves** or s-curves. Compound curves are formed of two oppositely turning curves.

2.10 Principle of Constructing Curves

A large number of the monoliterals are constructed using compound curves. Difficulty in scribing them fluently commonly occur because of incorrect curve construction. This is especially true with hieroglyphs of birds such as the owl, vulture and the quail chick where it is not uncommon to encounter depictions of birds exhibiting extremities of either inflated or narrow frontals. Perfecting the ability to reproduce realistic curves requires one to understand how varying curvatures are constructed. For example, given an illustration of the compound curve in fig. 2.9, how can it be reproduced accurately?

Using the principle of curve construction by Harold Speed (1913), we can reproduce this curve correctly by working out:

- How high is the curve; where does the curve **start** and **end**?

- At what point(s) does a **change in curvature** occurs from one direction to the other? This is only applicable when concerning compound curves.

- What is the highest point (**vertex**) of the curve?

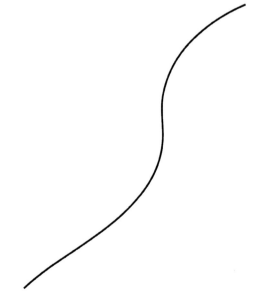

Fig. 2.9

1) Where are the start and end points of the curve? In this case they are marked with dots as A and B respectively.

The height of the curve will be the vertical distance between the two (start and end) points which is marked with the dotted line **AD**. The with of the curve is the horizontal distance between the two (start and end) points which is marked with the dotted line **BD**.

2) At what point(s) does a change in curvature occur? Note the point(s) at which the curvature changes direction. In this instance, there is only one point (**C**) marked with a dot.

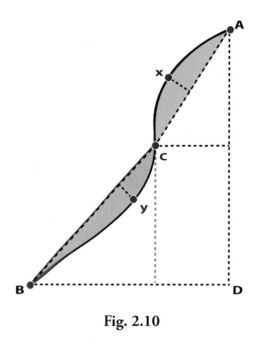

Fig. 2.10

3) What is the vertex (highest) point of the curve(s)?
Examine the first curve (blue) extending from points A to C. Estimate the vertex (highest) point of the curve. Mark it with a dot (**x**).

Examine the second (orange) curve and do the same (**y**).

The curvature can then be reproduced accurately by carefully connecting the five (**A-x-C-y-B**) dotted points together in the sequence.

In the beginning, you will need to note and mark each point but as you get better, it should be fairly easy to visualize the vertical and horizontal guidelines and compare them to the curve you are to draw.

Curve Estimation Challenge

Fig 2.11 shows an outline of a vase proportioned in a four by four grid. By using the principle of curve construction, how can the right side (orange curve) of the vase's outline be reproduced correctly?

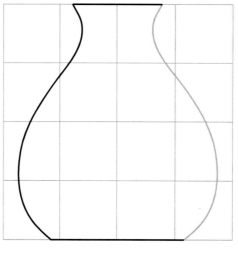

Fig. 2.11

Solution

1) Where are the start and end points of the curve? In this case they are marked with dots as **A** and **D** respectively.

The height of the curve will be the vertical distance between the two (start and end) points which is marked with the blue dotted line **AB**. The with of the curve is the horizontal distance between the two (start and end) points which is marked with the orange dotted line **BD**.

2) At what point(s) does a change in curvature occurs? It is marked with a dot as the point (**C**).

3) Where is the vertex (highest) point both curves? They are marked with the dots (**x**) and (**y**).

Connect all the dots (A-x-C-y-D) accordingly to create the compound curve.

Applying the same method in order to reproduce the right side of the vase making sure that the lines are connected at the correct points within the grid.

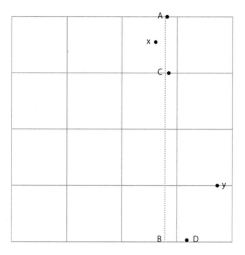

Fig. 2.12

2.11 Art Principles

Proportion or Scale

Scale and proportion both deal with size. **Scale** refers to the relationship between two or more objects size in an artwork. A single object has no scale until it is compared with something else. **Proportion** refers to the relative size of parts of an object in relationship to other parts (a whole) of the same object. Proportion is concerned with different sizes in objects being in agreement and balance. When one element changes in size, the others should also change size in similar proportion.

Nykemet art used what is known as *Hierarchical proportion* to emphasis that which was deemed important based on status or meaning by proportioning or scaling it larger than other accompanying objects.

Balance

This is the distribution of the visual weight in an artwork. Balance places parts in an aesthetically pleasing arrangement. There are three types of balance. In **symmetrical** balance, the elements on one side are similar to those on the other side (see fig 2.11); in **asymmetrical** balance, the elements on both sides are not identical but are arranged so that they have equal visual weight or sense of balance; In **radial** balance, the elements are arranged around a central point.

Shape

Shape is the outline of a two dimensional object and is created when a line is enclosed. Shapes with boundaries made from straight lines are known as **rectilinear.** Those made from curved lines are known as **curvilinear** whiles **compound** forms exhibit both straight and curved lines (see fig 2.6).[28]

Space

Space is the internal and external area an object occupies. The internal area occupied by the object is known as *positive space*. The the external or empty space between and around the objects such as a background is known as *negative space*.

Shape and space are closely linked in that, the shape of an object is implied by the use of both its internal and external space. Shapes cannot exist without space. This interrelationship is often used to produce optical illusion images (see fig 2.13). Two different shapes can be obtained depending on what is viewed as positive and negative space: either two faces in profile (black) or a vase (white).

Line, shape and space have a symbiotic relationship. They all help create each other in a visual composition.

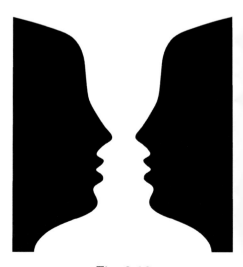

Fig. 2.13

_____

28   Walker, *Handbook of drawing*, p. 24

2.12 Tools

Paper

Knowing what paper to select can be a bit of a challenge considering the wide variety of choices available in the market. For simplification purposes, here are some of the requirements to keep in mind when selecting suitable paper.

Paper Surface - The paper surface should be smooth such that the tip of the nib does not pick up fibers when scribing. Smooth surfaces also help produce even lines.

Absorbency - To avoid ink bleed, choose papers with low absorbency level. They are processed to block ink absorption by making sure that the ink sits on the paper surface.

Archival - Acid free, neutral PH papers are excellent for projects meant to last without the paper yellowing over time.

Ink

Inks are used for drawing and writing. In the old days, carbon or soot mixed with water and a binding agent such as gum arabic was used to make ink. Today we use inks made from dyes or pigments. Inks made from dyes are usually used with fountain pens. They are thinner in consistency. Pigment-based inks are generally recommended for dip pens or brushes. On fountain pens they may clog the pen's feed and or the nib. Make sure you select the right ink for the tool you are to use.

Fountain Pen

A fountain pen is a writing instrument that draws ink from its internal reservoir through a feed to the nib and deposits it on paper by means of gravity and capillary action. The fountain pen's predecessor is the dip pen which requires constant dipping of its nib in an ink jar for every few written lines.

2.13 Parts of a Fountain Pen

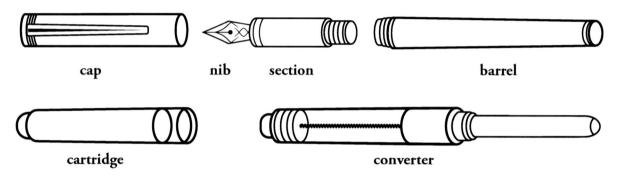

cap   nib   section   barrel

cartridge   converter

Fig. 2.14

When disassembled, the fountain pen consists of four main parts: the cap, the nib, the ink reservoir and the barrel.

The **cap** covers the nib and attaches to the body of the pen.

The **feed** is the black plastic at the bottom of the nib that gives way for the ink to go through from the ink reservoir. It also helps the air fill the container.

The **section** connects the feed to the ink.

Ink **reservoir** holds ink that is filled to the pen. The reservoir may be a **converter** or an ink **cartridge**.

Converters can either be piston/rotation or press squeeze/plate converter.

The cartridge is a self-contained, disposable unit filled with ink. The ink cartridge is preferred for its convenience but limited in the ink choices. On the hand, pens with converters allow for flexibility in ink color choices available.

When purchasing your pen, be mindful that not all fountain pens are designed with universal cartridge or converter fittings in mind. Certain manufacturers only utilize their own proprietary ink cartridges or converters.

Nib is the sharp metal tip of the fountain pen that touches the paper. Nibs come in varying shapes, sizes and flexibility. Different styles of writing calls for different types of nibs. The three basic shapes are round, stub, and italic. The most common is the round shape. It provides even strokes on paper. Stub and italic nibs are mainly used in calligraphy.

The five basic nib sizes are extra fine (**XF**), fine (**F**), medium (**M**), broad (**B**), and double broad (**BB**). **Fine** and **extra fine** sizes are ideal for scribing.

Note that nib tip sizes vary from one manufacture to the other such that not all nibs labeled with the same nib size produce the same line width when used.

2.14 Anatomy of a Nib

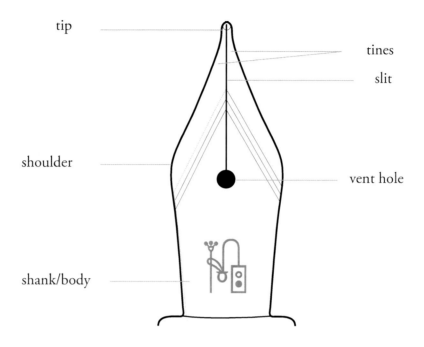

tip

tines

slit

shoulder

vent hole

shank/body

Fig. 2.15

- **Tip/point**: the sharpest point of the nib that contacts the paper.

- **Slit**: the gap between the two tines. The slit allows for ink to flow down to the paper through capillary action.

- **Tines**: two sides of the nib divided by the slit. On flexible nibs, they separate based on pressure, creating varied thick and thin strokes.

- **Shoulder**: this is where the pen transitions from the shank to the tip.

- **Vent hole**: acts as an ink reservoir by regulating the amount of ink flow. It also stops the division of the two tines by managing tension put on the tines to avoid the nib from splitting.

- **Shank**: supports and holds the nib in the pen holder.

- **Tail/base**: the part inserted into the section.

2.15 Filling of Fountain Pen with Ink

For piston converters, dip the nib and part of the section of the fountain pen into the bottle of ink (see fig 2.16) and turn the piston converter counterclockwise to force air out. Twist the top of the piston converter clockwise to suction up ink into the converter. Wipe the nib off with a lint-free cloth and reassemble the pen.

For squeeze converters, squeeze the air out of the converter before dipping it into the ink bottle. Release to suck in the ink. Remove the fountain pen from the ink bottle and wipe the nib off with a lint-free cloth. Reassemble the pen.

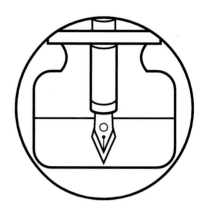

Fig. 2.16

Inserting a Cartridge

Insert the stopper end of the cartridge into the grip section of the pen. Firmly, press down the cartridge until it is punctured to allow for ink flow. Assemble the rest of the parts together. Place your pen in an upright position with its nib facing down and wait a few minutes for the ink to flow to the nib before using.

Cleaning the Fountain Pen

Clean your fountain pen when clogged or once a month. To do so, simply remove any excess ink from the ink converter.

Remove the converter from the bottom half (nib and feed) section of the pen.

Rinse the nib and feed section of the pen with tepid water until the water runs clear. Do the same for the converter by twisting and turning it in running tepid water to let the water in and out until it runs clear.

Drain and dry the parts with a lint free cloth/towel.

Never use hot water or solvents as they can damage the nib, finish and/or mechanism.

Storing the Fountain Pen

If the fountain pen is not to be used for a prolonged period of time, clean the pen and store with the nib in an upright position. This drains any residue ink from the nib into the refill.

2.16 Sitting Position

Sit upright with balanced shoulders. Do not slump or sit back with your body rested against the back of the chair.

Your feet should be evenly spaced and firmly planted flat on the floor to support the body.

Sitting height should allow for the writing forearm to rest on the table with the elbow free to pivot.

If the chair does not allow for height adjustments, cushion(s) can be added on the seat as substitute.

The work table should be large enough to place your working tools and accommodate comfortable arm movements.

The position of your paper in relation to you and the table should be comfortable without adding extra strain to your body.

Your elbow and forearm should lie on the desk when scribing while the other forearm is used to orient the paper and to keep it firm on the table.

2.17 Pen-hold

The pen can be held with either its cap posted (attached to the pen's barrel) or unposted. Most people prefer holding the pen posted for better balance. Those with smaller hands may prefer to leave the cap off. Hold the pen loosely between the tip of the thumb and the long bone of the index finger while letting it rest on the second (middle) finger. The hand should rest on the nails of the third (ring) and fourth (pinky) fingers which provide a gliding rest for it to move upon (see fig. 2.17).[29]

The pen should be held upright at about a 45 degree angle from the paper with the engraving on the nib facing up. Both tines at the tip of the nib should contact the paper simultaneously. Keep your wrist above the paper and make sure that you do not press the pen too tight. It should relax on the hand loosely. Tight grips will result in fatigue and an overall stressful scribing experience.

Practice on improving your pen-hold technique before commencing on any actual scribing.

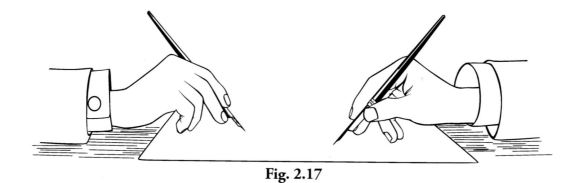

Fig. 2.17

2.18 Movement

Scribing is mechanically executed from separate but combined muscular action of the fingers, wrist, forearm and whole-arm (shoulder). Your skill level will not only depend on how well you have ingrained the shapes of the hieroglyphs in your mind, but also on how well you can control the right muscles in perfect balance for the task of producing the hieroglyphs accurately.

---

29   *Theory of the Spencerian System of Practical Penmanship*, Pck ed, Grand Rapids, MI, Mott Media 1985, p.4

Finger Movement

When using finger movement, action is applied from the index finger (downward strokes) and the middle finger (upward strokes). This muscle group is used for marking smaller details. Note that relying solely on this muscle group for scribing is not recommended. It can result in finger cramps and just overall poor penmanship. The fingers should ideally be tasked with holding the pen and applying pressure.

Wrist Movement

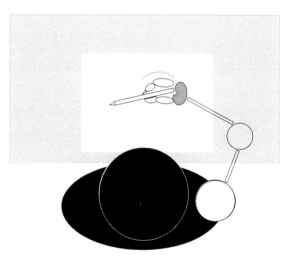

Fig. 2.18

With the forearm rested on the table, movement is applied from the wrist which acts as a fulcrum. Detailed and clearer strokes are produced and movement is much faster than those of the finger muscles. There is also a smoother transition between the wrist, forearm and whole arm muscles. However, this movement allows for scribing to occur only across a small surface area. The elbow must be used to move the wrist across the paper.

Forearm Movement

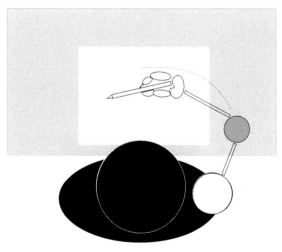

Fig. 2.19

The forearm muscle is situated right below the elbow. When using this muscle group, the elbow acts as a fulcrum. Forearm movement allows for coverage of a wider surface across the paper while still maintaining precision.

Whole Arm Movement

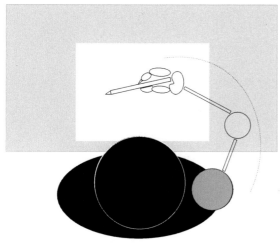

Whole arm is used to execute more elaborate and larger strokes. Movement is exerted from the shoulders while the elbow is lifted off the table to a degree.[30] Here the entire arm moves while the other parts are stable. Those who write on blackboards use this muscle group.

Fig. 2.20

Different stroke require execution from specific muscle groups. You will need to find a comfortable middle ground between the different muscular movements to help you scribe comfortably.

2.19 Drills

These drills are designed to:

- Develop simple muscular movements of different muscle groups when scribing.

- Maintain proper muscle group coordination to relieve tension.

- Attain effortless motion when scribing.

- Draw steady lines.

Use a pencil for drills 1 & 2. When comfortable, progress to the use of pens. **The wrist and fingers should not act when performing all the drills 1-3.**

30   Ibid, p.7

Drill 1 (drawing straight lines)

Place your pen/pencil at the point at which you wish to commence drawing the line.

Your gaze should be set at the point you wish to end the line.

Move your arm to draw the line.

Practice making a few lines (horizontal, vertical & oblique) of the same length and same distance apart daily until you can do them evenly.

Drill 2 (drawing circles)

Make overlapping circles in a clockwise motion Use your shoulders (whole arm movement) to control the motion. Practice making a few circles each of different sizes daily until you can do them evenly.

Drill 3 (air writing)

Bring your arm out in front of you with the elbow bent and write *legible* letters or draw objects in the air.

Start your scribing sessions with at least five to ten minutes of drills.

Exercise 2

1. Which of the statements is true?

    A. There was a clear distinction between drawing and writing in Kemet.

    B. Images accompanying texts in inscriptions were purely for decorative purposes.

    C. Images and texts were produced in adherence to conventions in Kemet.

    D. Images such as sculptures did not require additional text to accompany them.

2. Nykemet art was sometimes used as large logographs to convey messages through the rebus principle.

    A. True

    B. False

3. Nykemet art utilized our modern perspective for the organization of shapes in space.

    A. True

    B. False

4. Which one of the following is not a straight line?

    A. Horizontal

    B. Vertical

C.   Oblique

D.   Curve

5.   When reconstructing the blue curve of the glass bowl illustrated below, the point at which the curvature changes from one direction to the other is required.

A.   True

B.   False

CHAPTER 3

3. Scribing

3.1 Monoliterals

Middle Egyptian has 25 mono-consonantal signs[31] that must be ingrained in the mind in order to acquire all the known sounds in the language. On their own, these signs could have been used to write down any word combination even though they were never used as such but rather in combination with other signs.

The monoliterals are also built upon the **acrophonic principle**. Each monoliteral sign represents the initial phoneme of the word on which the pictorial sign is based. For example the consonant /d/ is depicted with the sign of a hand which is known as $\overline{\smile}$ *drt* ' deret' « hand » pronounced with its initial "d". This is why they are commonly viewed as the Kemety "alphabet".

Signs	Code	Description	Diacritic	MdC
	G1	Vulture	i	i
	M17	Reed Leaf	w	w
	M17+M17	Double Reed Leaf	r	r
	D36	Arm	$ʿ$	a
	G43	Quail Chick	w	w
	D58	Foot	b	b
	Q3	Stool Of Reed Mat	p	p
	I9	Horned Viper	f	f
	G17	Owl	m	m
	N35	Water Ripple	n	n
	D21	Mouth	r	r
	O4	Enclosure	h	h
	V28	Twisted Flax	$ḥ$	H
	Aa1	Placenta	$ḫ$	x
	F32	Belly and Udder	$ẖ$	X
	O34	door Bolt	z	z
	S29	Folded Cloth	s	s
	N37	Pool	$š$	S

---

31   The 25th mono-consonantal sign is the double reed leaf.

Signs	Code	Description	Diacritic	MdC
△	N29	Hill	k	q
⌣	V31	Basket with Handle	k	k
▲	W11	Jar Stand	g	g
⌒	X1	Raised Bread Loaf	t	t
⌓	V13	Tethering Rope	$\underline{t}$	T
⌒	D46	Hand	d	d
⌐	I10	Cobra in Repose	$\underline{d}$	D

Now that you have learned how to produce proper lines and use the correct muscle movements to scribe, we are going to combine these two techniques in order to create shapes that form simple outline drawings. The four types of lines (vertical, horizontal, oblique and curved) you have learned so far are all that are needed to scribe. Below are three examples of monoliterals broken down into the four basic lines used to produce their shapes. A good practice, is to break down each glyph to its basic lines before combining the strokes.

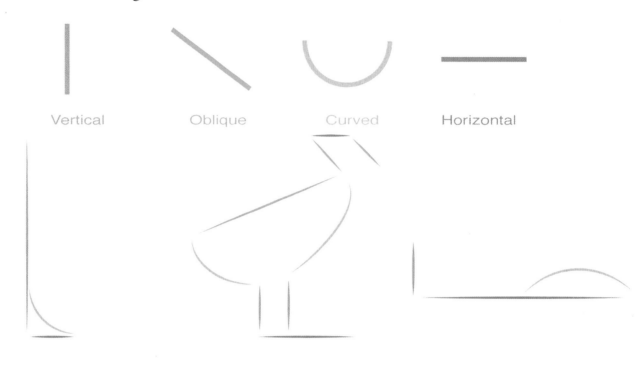

Vertical   Oblique   Curved   Horizontal

Fig. 3.1

Variations in lines occur in oblique and curved lines in regard to their angles and curvatures respectively. Curves tend to be the most difficult to draw but can be tackled with less difficulty once you are able to execute correct curve constructions.

In the next section, we will go over each individual monoliteral hieroglyph. Practice scribing each one correctly before moving on to the next. The forms of hieroglyphs presented are close models of those found in the *papyrus of Ani*. Considerations are taken into account on the adherence of the shape each individual hieroglyph may take in a quadrat block. Slight modifications are also done to accommodate the tools used which differ from those used by the scribes of Kemet. All simplified hieroglyphs are illustrated facing right.

Having a clear visual image of a hieroglyph should be coupled with the ability to reproduce it accurately from memory. A scribe aims at fluency and mastery of each glyph so as to be able to reproduce its every stroke and combine them to perfect order.

3.2 VULTURE

Gardiner code: G1

Identification: Egyptian Vulture (Neophron percnopterus)

Pronunciation (Egyptology Speak): "a" as in father.

Vulture (simplified)

Strokes: 2

Pen lifts: 1

Shape: Tall Narrow

Notes:

- The beak starts at the middle of square **A1**'s height.

- The hind leg should ideally be at a 1/3 of the height of square **D4** or slightly lower.

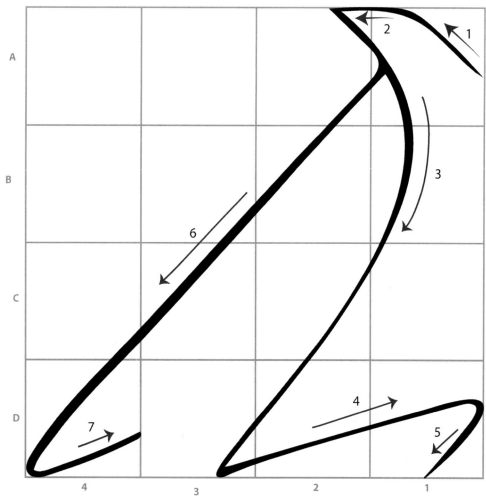

3.3 REED LEAF

Gardiner code: M17

Identification: Read Leaf

Pronunciation (Egyptology Speak): "ee" as in feet.

Reed Leaf (simplified)

Strokes: 2

Pen lifts: 1

Shape: Tall Narrow

Notes:

• The last stroke (**arrow 4**) sits at the middle of the leaf's height and can be made straight but is ideally slightly curved.

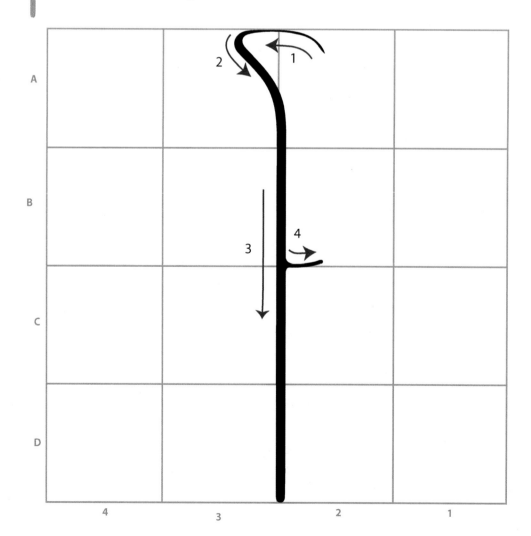

3.4 DOUBLE REED LEAF

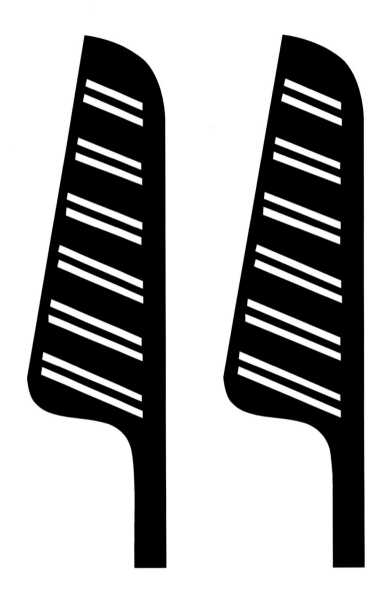

Gardiner code: M17 + M17

Identification: Double Read Leaf

Pronunciation (Egyptology Speak): "ee" as in sleep.

Double Reed Leaf (simplified)

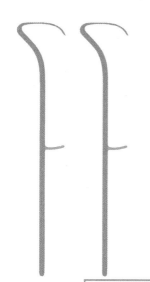

Tall Narrow

Strokes: 4

Pen lifts: 3

Shape: Tall Narrow

Notes:

- This is a doubling of the previous read leaf.

- If you feel confident with your line production skills, try scribing the read leaves within the squares as shown below and not on the line axis. Otherwise, use the axis as guides when scribing them.

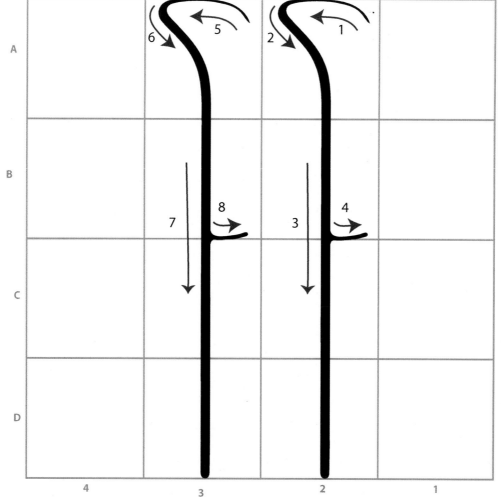

3.5 ARM

Gardiner code: D36

Identification: Arm

Pronunciation (Egyptology Speak): "a" as in father.

Arm (simplified)

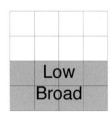

Low
Broad

Strokes: 1

Pen lifts: 0

Shape: Low Broad

Notes:

- This glyph is drawn from start to finish in one stroke (no pen lift) until the end of the curve which rests at the bottom left corner of square **C2.**

- Practice making each individual line (vertical, horizontal and curve) separately and then in combination in order to form the glyph.

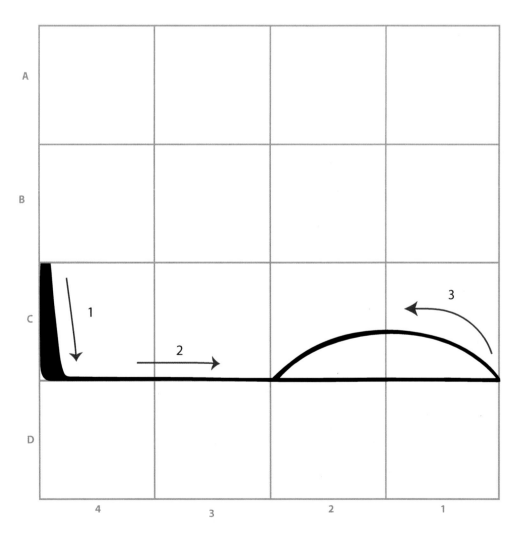

3.6 QUAIL CHICK

Gardiner code: G43

Identification: Quail Chick

Pronunciation (Egyptology Speak): at the beginning of a word like English w as in 'one', otherwise, "oo" as in too.

Quail Chick (simplified)

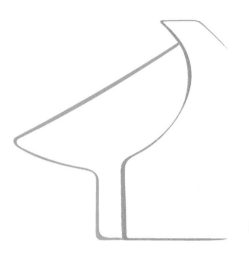

Tall Narrow

Strokes: 2

Pen lifts: 1

Shape: Tall Narrow

Notes:

- The head of the bird is drawn similarly to that of the vulture.

- Pay close attention to where the vertex point of the curve lies (**arrow 3**).

- The hind leg (**arrow 8**) starts at a lower height than the front leg (**arrow 4**).

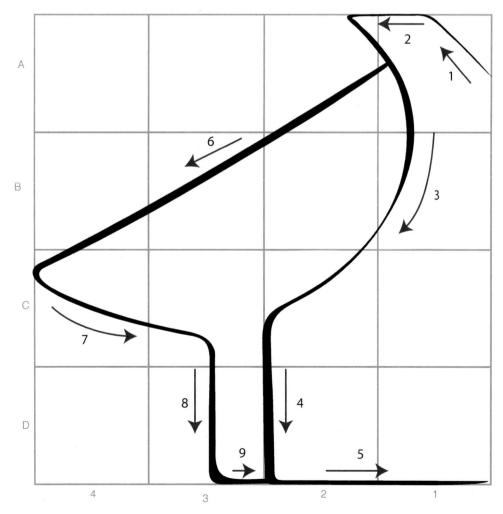

3.7 FOOT

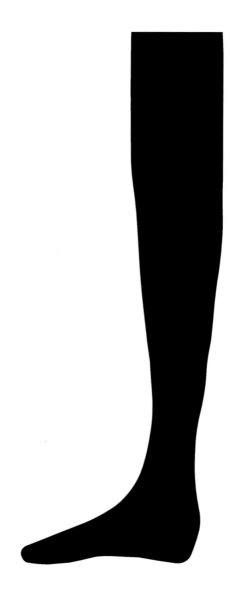

Gardiner code: D58

Identification: Foot

Pronunciation (Egyptology Speak): b as boy.

Foot (simplified)

Tall Narrow

Strokes: 1

Pen lifts: 0

Shape: Tall Narrow

Notes:

- This glyph is drawn from start to finish in one stroke (no pen lift) until the end of the curve (**arrow 3**).

- Make sure that your lines are not shaky. Practice making each individual line (vertical, horizontal and curve) separately and then combine them to form the glyph.

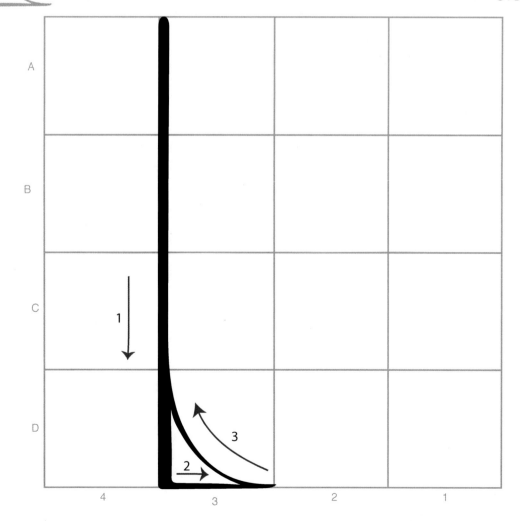

3.8 STOOL OF REED MAT

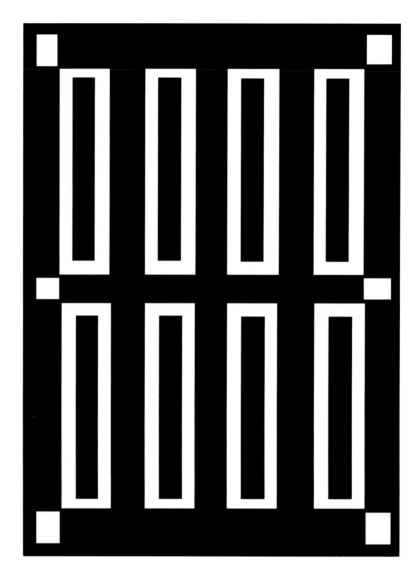

Gardiner code: Q3

Identification: Stool of Reed Mat

Pronunciation (Egyptology Speak): p as in pot.

Stool of Reed Mat (simplified)

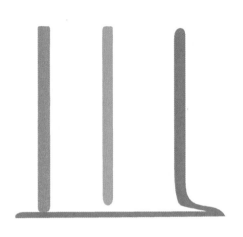

Low
Narrow

Strokes: 3

Pen lifts: 2

Shape: Low Narrow

Notes:

- The vertical line (**arrow 3**) can be drawn without the accent connecting it to the horizontal line (**arrow 4**) but for the sake of speed, the joining stroke is added.

- When scribed without the joining stroke, the glyph consists of three vertical lines placed on top of a horizontal line.

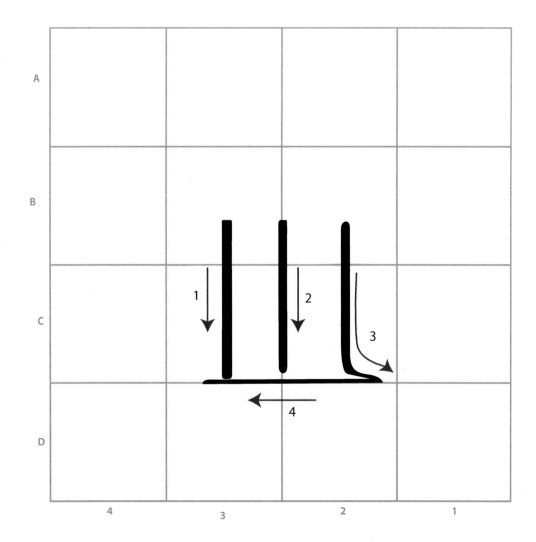

3.9 HORNED VIPER

Gardiner code: I9

Identification: Horned Viper

Pronunciation (Egyptology Speak): f as in fire.

Horned Viper (simplified)

Strokes: 2

Pen lifts: 1

Shape: Low Broad

Notes:

- The first stroke that makes up the horned viper's body resembles a lower case "w" letter that is stretched out.

- The final stroke (**arrow 2**) sits at an angle of about 90° forming the viper's horns.

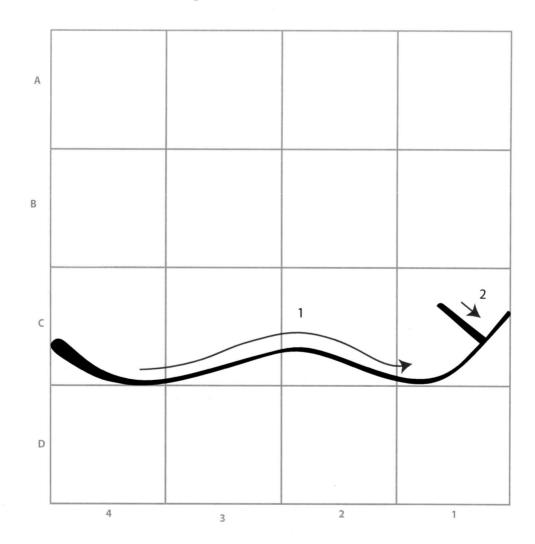

3.10 OWL

Gardiner code: G17

Identification: Owl

Pronunciation (Egyptology Speak): m as in more.

Owl (simplified)

Tall Narrow

Strokes: 3

Pen lifts: 2

Shape: Tall Narrow

Notes:

- The last stroke (**arrow 7**) is perpendicular to the opposite oblique stroke (**arrow 1**). It sits at about 90 ° angle to form the owl's head.

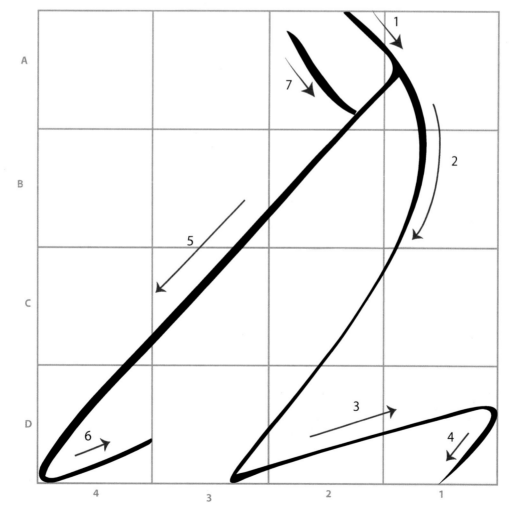

3.11 WATER RIPPLE

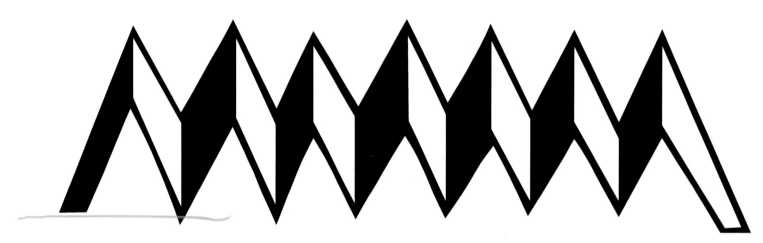

Gardiner code: N35

Identification: Water Ripple

Pronunciation (Egyptology Speak): n as in no.

Water Ripple (simplified)

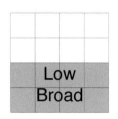

Notes:

- This is an easy glyph to scribe. Make sure the line is not shaky.

- Simply draw a straight horizontal line, straight across.

Strokes: 1

Pen lifts: 0

Shape: Low Broad

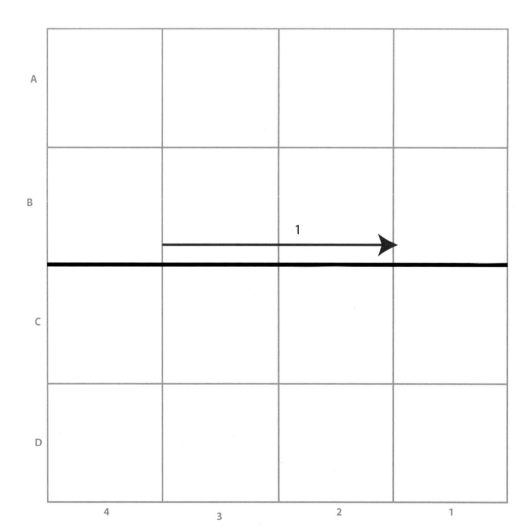

3.12 MOUTH

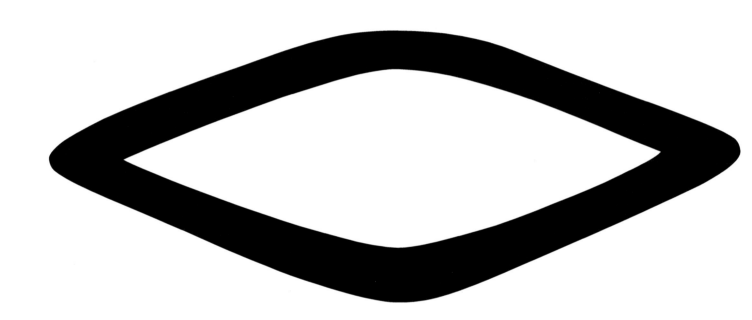

Gardiner code:D22

Identification: Water Ripple

Pronunciation (Egyptology Speak): r as in rain.

Mouth (simplified)

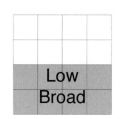

Strokes: 1

Pen lifts: 0

Shape: Low Broad

Notes:

- This glyph consists of two similar curves at opposite placement.
- The vertex of each curve is at the mid point of the grid's full width.

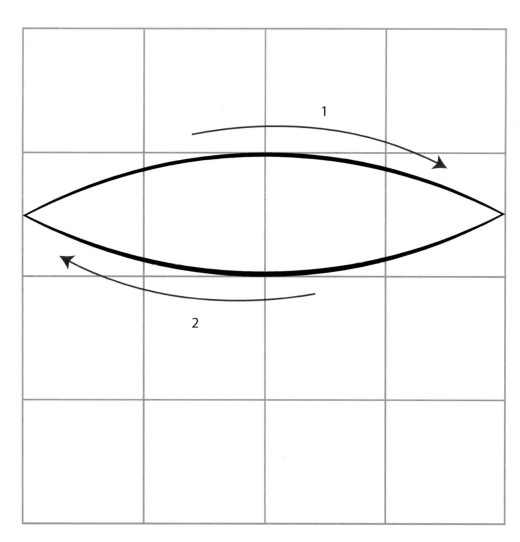

3.13 ENCLOSURE

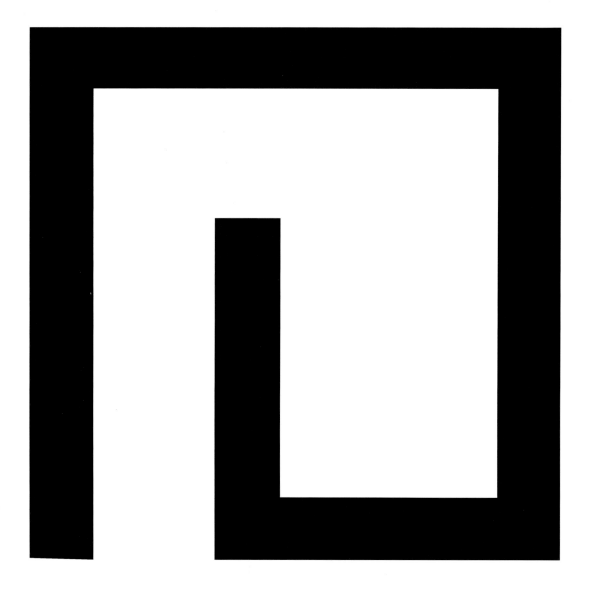

Gardiner code: O4

Identification: Enclosure

Pronunciation (Egyptology Speak): h as in here.

Enclosure (simplified)

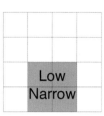

Low Narrow

Strokes: 1

Pen lifts: 0

Shape: Low Narrow

Notes:

- The glyph consists of vertical and horizontal lines executed in one stroke.

- Practice making the different vertical and horizontal lines separately before scribing the glyph in one full execution.

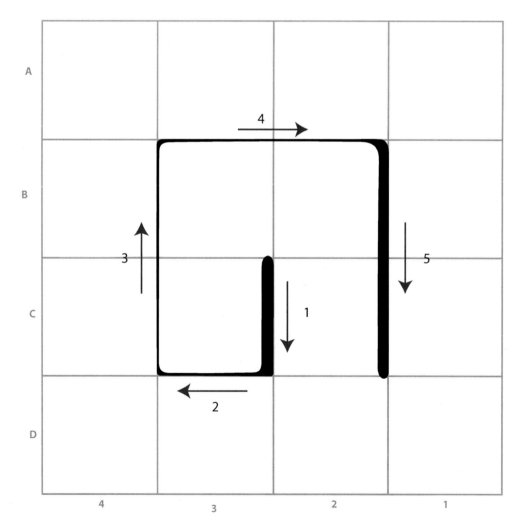

3.14 TWISTED FLAX

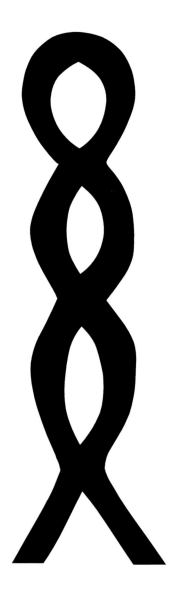

Gardiner code: V28

Identification: Twisted Flax

Pronunciation (Egyptology Speak): like a very airy English h Asian hot - example: *ḥnꜥ* "with," pronounced "HEN-ah".

Twisted Flax (simplified)

Strokes: 6

Pen lifts: 5

Shape: Tall Narrow

Notes:

- The top section is of an oval shape with the tail extending out perpendicular to the oblique strokes marked as **arrows 2, 3,4** and **5.**

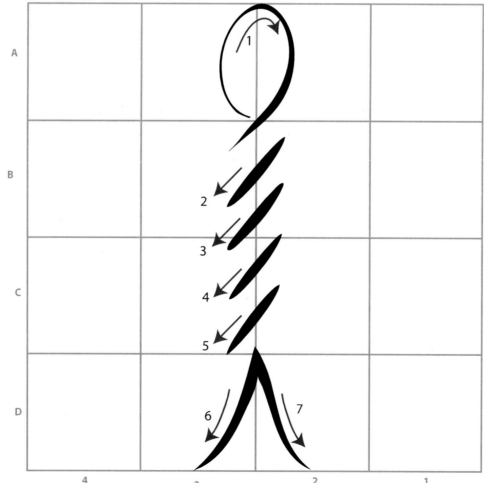

3.15 PLACENTA

Gardiner code: Aa1

Identification: Placenta

Pronunciation (Egyptology Speak): Hard k as if clearing throat like the kh sound in German ach or Scottish loch- example ḫbỉ "dance", pronounced "KHEB-ee".

Placenta (simplified)

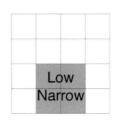

Low
Narrow

Notes:

- The circle covers the area of a 2*2 grid.
- The three oblique strokes are added at the circle's center.

Strokes: 4

Pen lifts: 3

Shape: Low Narrow

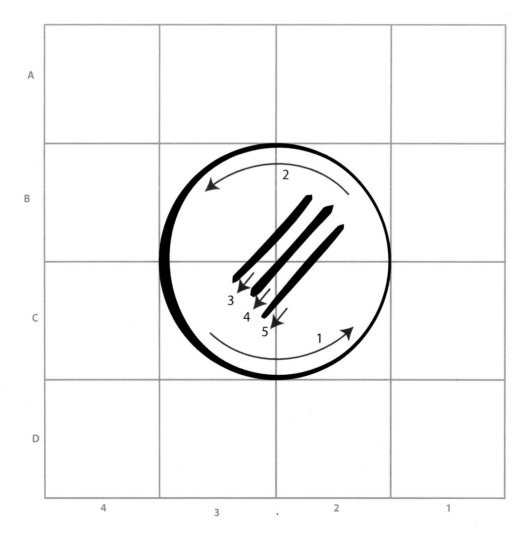

3.16 BELLY AND UDDER

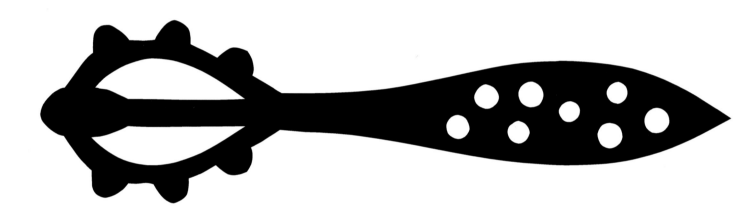

Gardiner code: F32

Identification: Bely and Udder

Pronunciation (Egyptology Speak): the kh sound followed by y or whispered h as in he - example Xrd "child", pronounced "KHYAH-red" or "KYAH-red".

Belly and Udder (simplified)

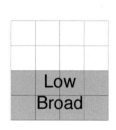

Low
Broad

Strokes: 6

Pen lifts: 5

Shape: Low Broad

Notes:

- This glyph consists of a straight horizontal line and an ellipse-like curve.

- Finish off by adding 4 vertical lines (**arrows 4, 5, 6 and 7**) as accents.

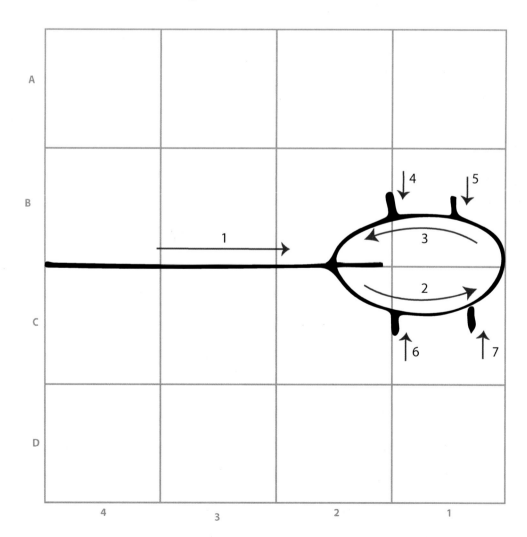

3.17 DOOR BOLT

Gardiner code: O34

Identification: Door Bolt

Pronunciation (Egyptology Speak): like English z or s: example *zỉ* "man," pronounced "zee" or "see".

Door Bolt (simplified)

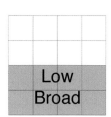

Strokes: 3

Pen lifts: 2

Shape: Low Broad

Notes:

- Simply draw a straight horizontal line straight across the 4*4 grid.

- The two parallel oblique lines should be evenly spaced apart at the center of the 4*4 grid.

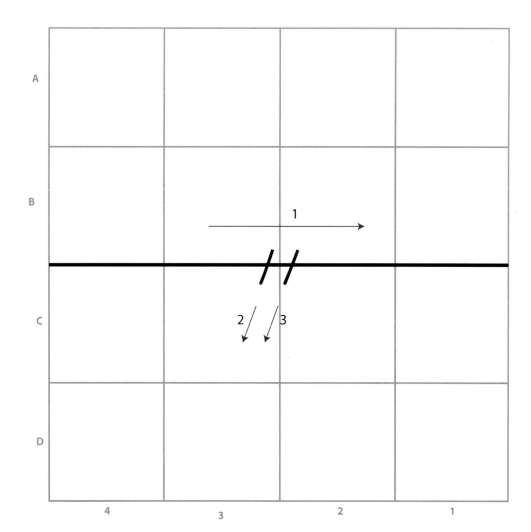

3.18 FOLDED CLOTH

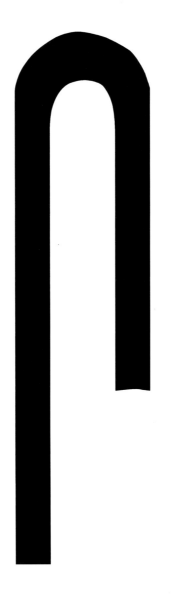

Gardiner code: S29

Identification: Folded Cloth

Pronunciation (Egyptology Speak): s as in sun.

Folded Cloth (simplified)

Strokes: 1

Pen lifts: 0

Shape: Tall Narrow

Notes:

- Make sure that both vertical lines (**arrows 1 & 3**) are straight.

- The curve (**arrow 2**) is symmetrical.

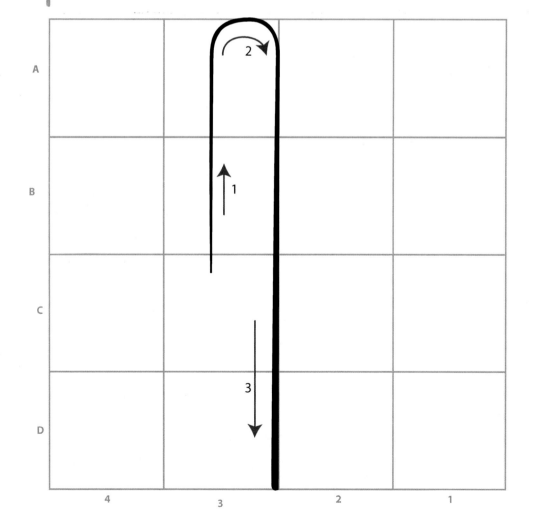

3.19 POOL

Gardiner code: N37

Identification: Pool

Pronunciation (Egyptology Speak): sh as in shoe.

Pool (simplified)

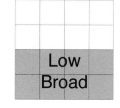

Strokes: 2

Pen lifts: 1

Shape: Low Broad

Notes:

- The glyph is scribed by drawing a rectangle (**arrows 1, 2, 3 & 4**) and a straight line (**arrow 5**) inside the rectangle.

- Practice making straight lines (vertical & horizontal) separately before making one full execution.

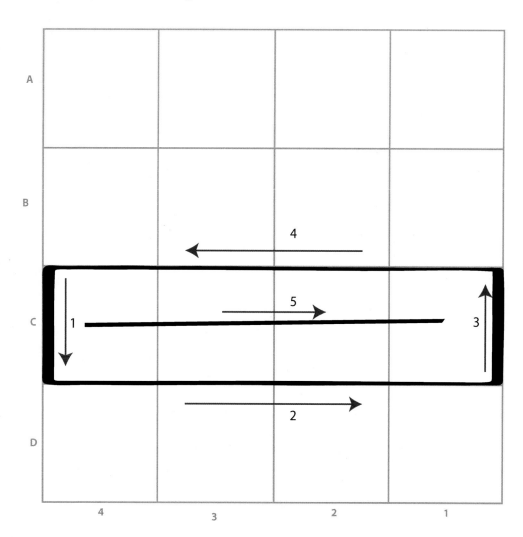

3.20 HILL

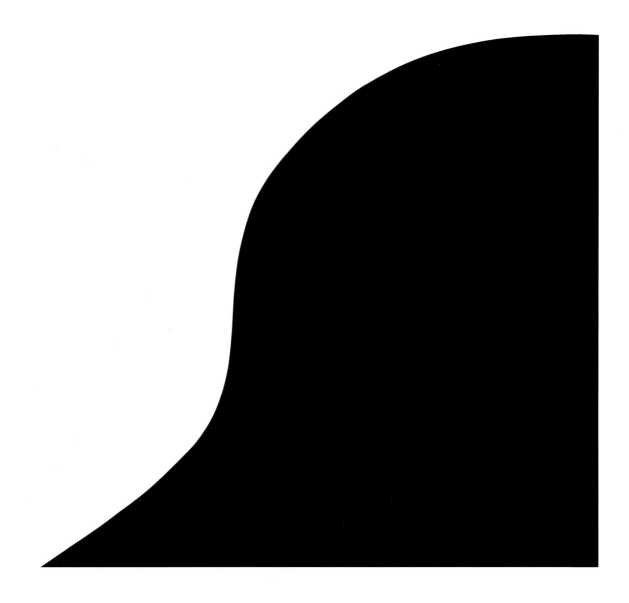

Gardiner code:: N29

Identification: Hill

Pronunciation (Egyptology Speak): "like English k in Keep.

Hill (simplified)

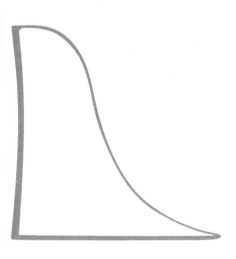

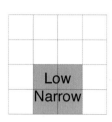

Low
Narrow

Strokes: 1

Pen lifts: 0

Shape: Low Narrow

Notes:

- Note that the first stroke (**arrow 1**) is not straight but slightly curved.

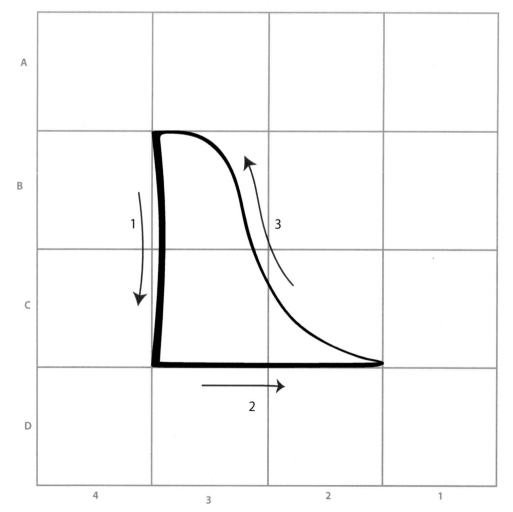

3.21 BASKET WITH HANDLE

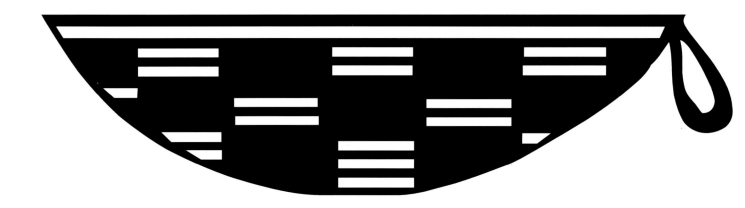

Gardiner code: V31

Identification: Basket with Handle

Pronunciation (Egyptology Speak): k as in kick.

Basket with Handle (simplified)

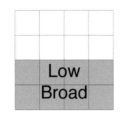

Low			
Broad			

Notes

Strokes: 1

Pen lifts: 0

Shape: Low Broad

- This variation of the basket with a handle is easier to execute.

- It consists of an oval section resembling a slanted letter "e" and a straight horizontal line.

- Make sure that your curves and straight lines are smooth.

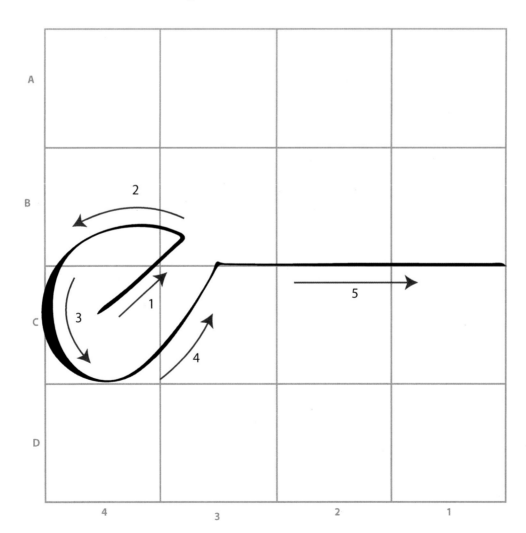

3.22 JAR STAND

Gardiner code: W11

Identification: Jar Stand

Pronunciation (Egyptology Speak): g as in get, go.

Jar Stand (simplified)

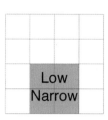

Low
Narrow

Strokes: 4

Pen lifts: 3

Shape: Low Narrow

Notes:

- The vertical line (**arrow 5**) can be drawn without the accent connecting it to the horizontal line (**arrow 6**) but for the sake of speed, the joining stroke is added.

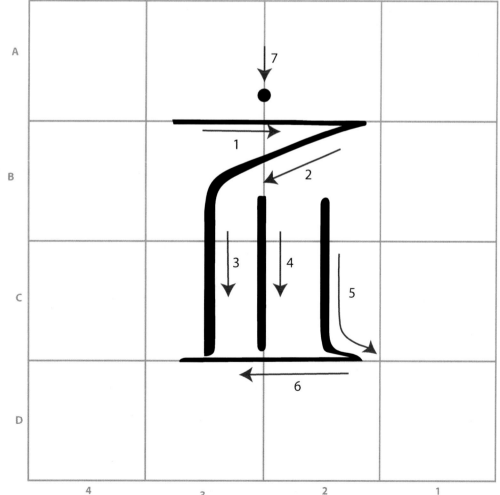

3.23 RAISED BREAD LOAF

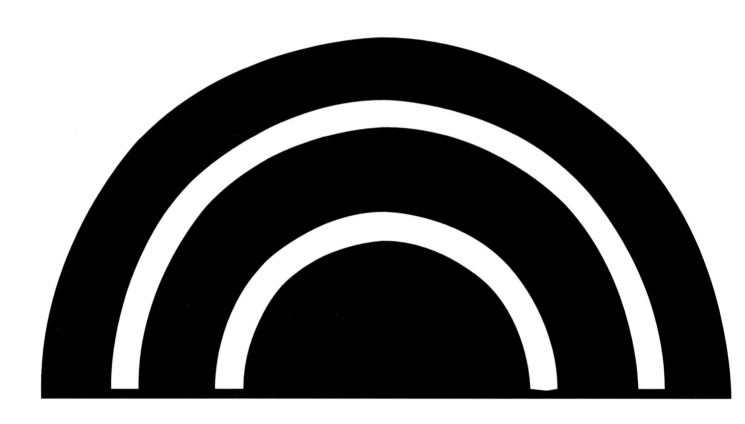

Gardiner code: X1

Identification: Raised Bread Loaf

Pronunciation (Egyptology Speak): t as in top.

Raised Bread Loaf (simplified)

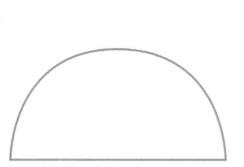

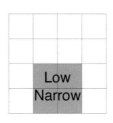

Notes:

- The glyph consists of a curved line **(arrow 1)** and a horizontal line **(arrow 2)**.

- The inner section is always shaded.

Strokes: 1

Pen lifts: 0

Shape: Low Narrow

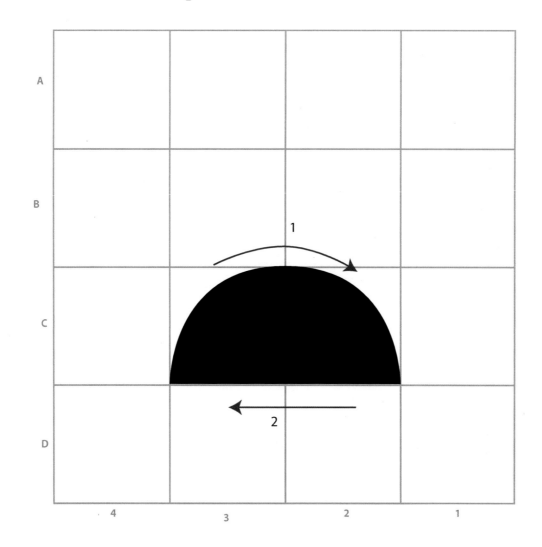

3.24 TETHERING ROPE

Gardiner code: V13

Identification: Tethering Rope

Pronunciation (Egyptology Speak): like English ch in church.

Tethering Rope (simplified)

Low		
Broad		

Strokes: 2

Pen lifts: 1

Shape: Low Broad

Notes:

- The glyph resembles the letter "u" laying down.

- Pay attention to the curved accents (**arrows 4 and 5**).

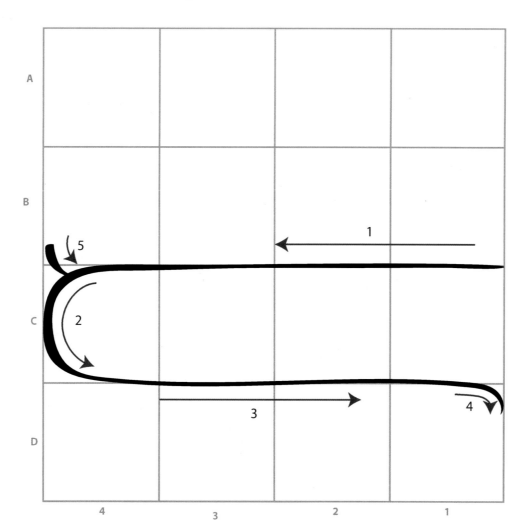

3.25 HAND

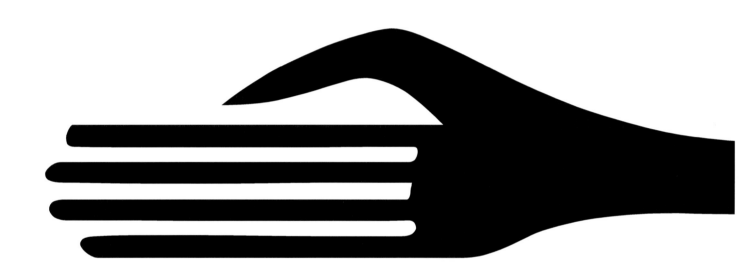

Gardiner code: D46

Identification: Hand

Pronunciation (Egyptology Speak): d as in do.

Hand (simplified)

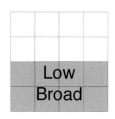

Low
Broad

Strokes: 2

Pen lifts: 1

Shape: Low Broad

Notes:

- For the first stroke, simply draw a straight horizontal line straight across the 4*4 grid.

- Note that the second stroke is a compound curve with a slight curvature at its beginning.

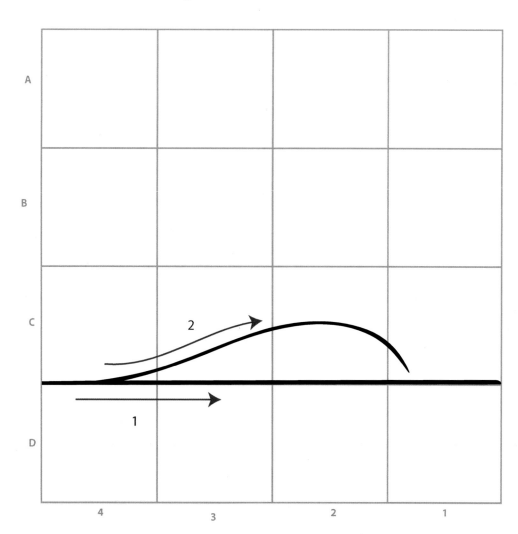

3.26 COBRA IN REPOSE

Gardiner code: I10

Identification: Cobra in Repose

Pronunciation (Egyptology Speak): like English j in judge.

Cobra in Repose (simplified)

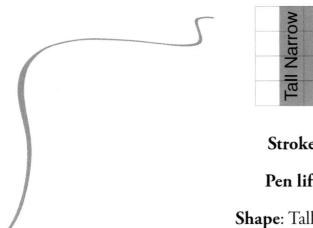

Tall Narrow

Strokes: 1

Pen lifts: 0

Shape: Tall Narrow

Notes:

- The stroke starts from the top corner to bottom left corner of the 4*4 grid.

- Make sure the different vertex points of the compound curves are situated in their correct positions.

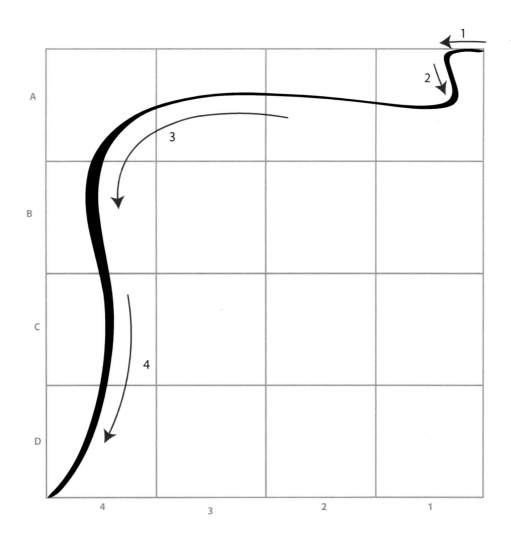

3.27 Variations

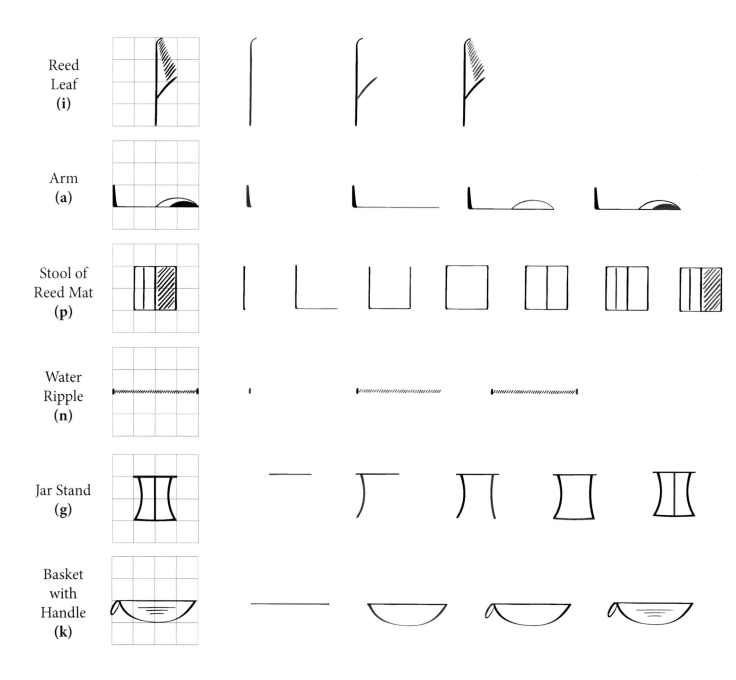

3.28 Monoliteral List

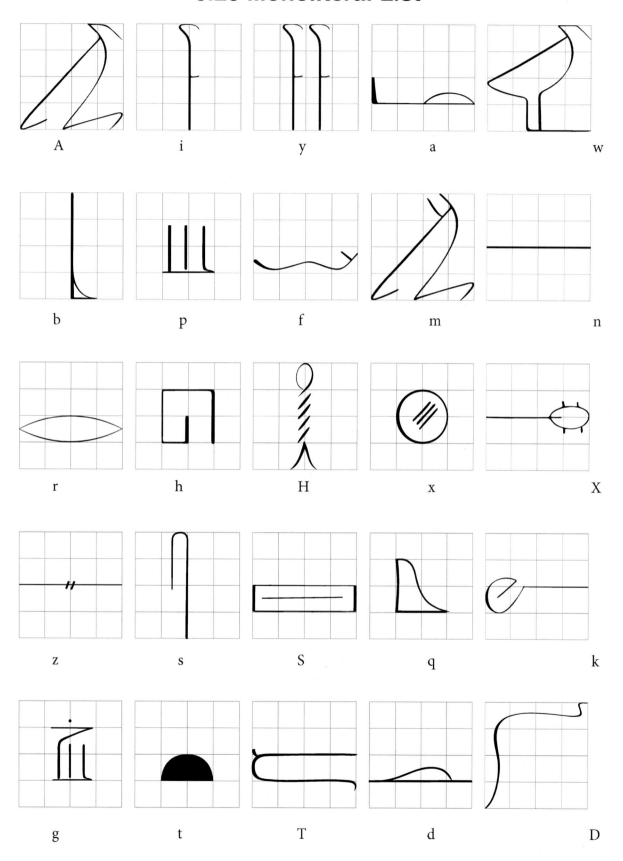

A	i	y	a	w
b	p	f	m	n
r	h	H	x	X
z	s	S	q	k
g	t	T	d	D

Exercise 3

1.   Scribe the name ra-ms-sw (**rameses**) below using the monoliterals.

2.   The following are transliterations (MdC) of Nykemet numbers. Can you scribe them using the monoliterals?

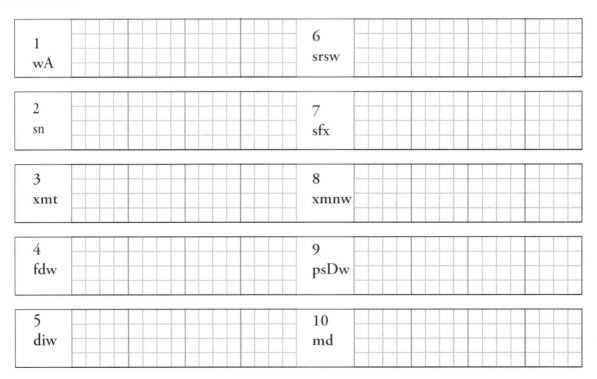

1 wA		6 srsw	
2 sn		7 sfx	
3 xmt		8 xmnw	
4 fdw		9 psDw	
5 diw		10 md	

3.   Scribe your name below using the monoliterals.

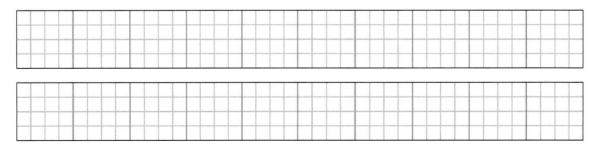

Appendices

Appendix 1: These are answers for the exercises in chapters 1 -3. They are constructed to act as a review of the concepts provided in this book.

Appendix 2: List of signs grouped according to the shapes each glyph occupy in a quadrat block, namely, Tall and narrow, Low and Broad, Low and Narrow.

Appendix 1: Exercise Solutions.

Exercise 1 Answers

1. Sesh Medew Netcher

2. Horizontal left to right (HLR).

3. False. Scribes adhered to conventions in their scribal methods by arranging the glyphs in an orderly and proportioned manner.

4. False. Ligatures can be found in Sesh Medjat Netcher (Hieratic) and Demotic scripts.

5. *sbꜣyt*

Exercise 2 Answers

1. Images and texts were produced in adherence to conventions in Kemet.

2. True

3. False. Nykemet art utilized what is known as *Aspective* to organize shapes in space.

4. Curve

5. False. This is a simple curve, not a compound curve. The following three are needed for its construction: the start point, end point and vertex (highest) point of the curve.

Exercise 3

1.

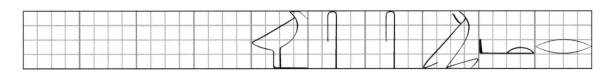

2.

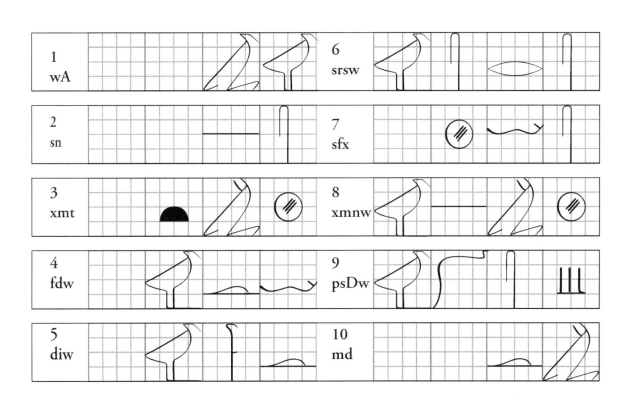

3. An example: My name is **Emykhet**. Pronounced "ee-mee-khet". Going by the sounds, it is spelled out using the monoliterals as **i-m-i-x-t** as scribed below.

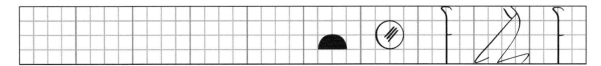

Appendix 2: Sign List

Tall and Narrow.

Aa20	Aa21	Aa25	Aa26	Aa27	Aa28	Aa29	Aa30	Aa31	Aa32
D16	F10	F11	F12	F28	F31	F35	F36	F45	H6
H6a	L7	M12	M13	M17	M29	M30	M32	M4	M40
M44	O11	O28	O30	O36	O44	P11	P6	P8	Q7
R11	R14	R15	R16	R17	R19	R21	R8	R9	S29
S34	S36	S37	S38	S39	S40	S41	S42	S43	S44
T13	T14	T15	T18	T19	T20	T22	T23	T3	T34
T35	T4	T7a	T8	T8a	U23	U24	U25	U26	U27
U28	U29	U32	U33	U34	U36	U39	U41	V17	V18
V24	V25	V28	V29	V36	V38	V39	W19	Y8	Z11

Low and Broad.

Aa10	Aa11	Aa12	Aa13	Aa14	Aa15	Aa24	Aa7	Aa8	Aa9
D13	D14	D15	D17	D21	D22	D24	D25	D48	D51
F18	F20	F30	F32	F33	F42	F46	F47	F48	F49
M11	N1	N11	N12	N16	N17	N18	N20	N30	N31
N35	N36	N37	N38	N39	O29	O31	O34	O42	O43
R22	R23	R24	R4	R5	R6	S12	S24	S32	T1
T10	T11	T2	T21	T30	T31	T33	T7	T9	T9a
U14	U15	U16	U17	U18	U19	U20	U21	U31	V13
V14	V16	V2	V22	V23	V26	V27	V3	V30	V31
V31a	V32	W3	W8	X4	X5	Y1	Y2	Z6	

Low and Narrow.

Aa1	Aa16	Aa17	Aa19	Aa2	Aa3	Aa4	D11	D12	D26
F21	F34	F38	F43	F51	F52	H8	I6	K6	L6
M31	M35	M36	M39	M41	M42	N10	N15	N21	N22
N23	N28	N29	N32	N33	N34	N41	N42	N5	N6
N8	N9	O39	O45	O46	O47	O48	O49	O50	Q3
R7	S10	S11	S20	S21	T28	U30	V1	V19	V20
V33	V34	V35	V37	V6	V7	V8	V9	W10	W10a
W11	W12	W13	W20	W21	W6	W7	X1	X2	X3
X6	X7	Y6	Z10	Z7	Z8	Z9			

References

Antelme, Schumann and Rossini (2002). *Illustrated Hieroglyphics Handbook, subsection - General Considerations on Hieroglyphic Writing,* New York, Sterling Publishing Co., Inc.

Budge, E. A Wallis (1973). *Easy Lessons in Egyptian Hieroglyphics with Sign List, vol 3,* London, Routledge & Kegan Paul Ltd.

Danijela, Stefanović (2012). *sS qdwt – The Attestations from the Middle Kingdom and the Second Intermediate Period* Budapest, Museum of Fine Arts.

Eyre, Christopher and Baines, John (1947). *Interactions between Orality and Literacy in Ancient Egypt,* edited by Karen Schousboe and Mogens. Trolle Larsen (eds),New York, London, Oxford University Press, Inc.

Gardiner, Alan H (1947). *Ancient Egyptian Onomastica, vol. 1,* New York, London, Oxford University Press, Inc.

Iry-Maat, Wudjau Men-Ib (2015). *A Beginner's Introduction to Medew Netcher,* Heka Multimedia.

Johnson, W. Martin (1909). *The W. Martin Johnson school of art, Elementary Instruction In Color, Perspective, Lights and Shadows - pen drawing and composition,* New York, Library of Congress.

Krispin, Arthur (2005). *An Overview of Ancient Egyptian Art , Anistoriton Journal,* section O054, Vol. 9.

Obenga, Theophile (2004). *African Philosophy, The Pharaonic Period: 2780-330 BC,* Per Ankh Publishing.

Oxford Advanced Learner's Dictionary (2010). (8th ed), Oxford, New York, Oxford University Press.

Robins, Gay (1994). *Proportion and Style in Ancient Egyptian Art,* Austin,TX, University of Texas Press.

Quirke, Stephen (2004). *Egyptian Literature 1800 BC, Questions and Readings,* London Golden

House Publications Egyptology 2.

Redford, Donald B ed., (2001). *The Oxford Encyclopaedia of Ancient Egypt,* vol 1, New York,. Oxford University Press, Inc.

Schafer, Heinrich (2002). *Principles of Egyptian Art,* ed. Emma Brunner-Traut, trans. and ed. John Baines.Oxford, U .K.: Griffith Institute Oxford.

Seshew Maa Ny Medea Netcher (2016). *Has the Egyptian Hieroglyphic Writing System Been Deciphered? - A Rebuttal to Walter Williams.*

Speed, Harold (1913). *The Practice & Science of Drawing,* London, Seeley, Service & Co. Limited.

Sullivan, Edmund J. (1922). *Line: An Art Study,* London, Chapman & Hall, Ltd.,

Theory of the Spencerian System of Practicle Penmanship. (1985) Pck ed, Grand Rapids, MI, Mott Media.

Walker, William (1880). *Handbook of drawing,* New York, C. Scribner's sons.

Wilkinson, Richard H (1992). *Reading Egyptian Art - A Hieroglyphic Guide to Ancient Egyptian Painting and Sculpture,* London: Thames and Hudson.

Williams, Ronald J (1972). *Scribal Training in Ancient Egypt,* JAOS Vol. 92, No. 2.

Made in the USA
Coppell, TX
20 October 2022